08/02/18

wut /8./8

CHURCH
ORGANIZATION

(561) 503-0456

CHURCH ORGANIZATION

JOSIAS MADISTIN

Xulon Press

Xulon Press
2301 Lucien Way #415
Maitland, FL 32751
407.339.4217
www.xulonpress.com

Scripture quotations taken from the King James Version (KJV) – *public domain.*

Scripture quotations taken from the American Standard Version (ASV)) – *public domain*

Scripture quotations taken from the New American Standard Bible (NASB). Copyright © 1960, 1962, 1963, 1968, 1971, 1972, 1973, 1975, 1977, 1995 by The Lockman Foundation. Used by permission. All rights reserved.

Scripture quotations taken from the Delphi Septuagint - Complete Greek and English Edition, by Publishdrive, Copyright © 2016.

Scripture quotations taken from the Fire Bible, by Hendrickson publishers, Copyright © 2010.

Edited by Xulon Press.

Printed in the United States of America.

ISBN-13: 9781545607879

CONTENTS

FOREWORD

I was not trained for writing. The challenges that I have encountered on the path of my ministry have prompted me to write these lines for a better management of the work of God.

I am not yet at the level where I dream to arrive.

Pastor Madistin, pastor of Elim church of God, Lantana, Florida, pastor missionary. Many people say that I am very sympathetic to people.

In the role of pastor missionary, I saw the miseries of our churches, diseases, and serious wounds.

I saw the wounds. Before going further, we must look at the reasons for these wounds, the reasons in the past, the reasons for the present condition.

The Church is known as a superpower. Many of the leaders of the evangelical end times have shaken the powers of the devil to encourage men to choose the path of God. After twenty-three years in the mission field, we can say that the **"ax"** is fallen in the water and we must go in search of it (2 Kings 6). We need to rediscover our Gospel.

I have always believed that the Church will overcome its enemies. Do not take me wrong, sometimes, I am worried and I cry for the bad news of the Church of Christ.

I believe the Church will raise to its standard until the return of our Lord and Savior Jesus Christ. I did not know my calling included to write until 2009, when God pushed me to this.

In this role, I must convince the churches of Christ that we are called upon to confess our problems. It is very hard to do, but we do not have a choice. I do not want to put myself above you, so my readers do not become angry with me. We must all work together to find solutions to these problems.

I think that if we apply biblical principles, the task will become easier. I am preparing to provide treatment. I do not say that it is excellent, but it will be able to help us if we need to raise the level of operation of the

Church. This fight, we will hold in a good conscience, a pure consciousness. As a minister of God, I am very confident that the Church will move forward. Despite the devastation of the church organization, we have the capacity to edify the Body of Christ. My brothers and sisters, have the courage to accomplish this noble task that we are called upon to fill. Do not sit down, let's stand to edify the Body of Christ. We can do as those who went before us as have done. We have the strength and courage, but we lack the determination. Those who wait on the Lord shall renew their strength; They shall mount up with wings like eagles; they shall run, and not be weary, they shall walk, and not faint (Isaiah 40.31). We will win the victory of our time.

I have always said 'The Church cannot die; impossible! Jesus said to Peter, "the gates of hell shall not prevail against it" (Matthew 16.18). The Church has need of our help to keep focused on Christ, the supreme chief of the Church. These are the seeds that I would like to sow in these days of famine. Called to the ministry by the grace of God, I am prepared by him to lead in the quest for these truths.

At the dawn of the third millennium, the marvels flow. The words of encouragement will be insufficient, because the task is immense. But I hope the minutes to come will bring life and strengthen us.

It is said, "It takes a village to raise a child." in this case, we need the whole Christian community to deal with the wounds. Let's fix the "ax" to continue to cut the wood required for the building. I refuse to put down the weapons. "Who shall separate us from the love of God?" We will continue to attack the wounds of the church with a huge desire to win. We will attack our personal work with this same mentality of a winner. It is a formula very large for the Church. The Apostle says to the Philippians: "I can do all things through Christ who strengthens me" (Phil. 4.13).

Pastor Josias Madistin,
Elim church of God
Lantana, Florida.

Introduction

1 Timothy 1.18-19
Timothy, my child, I am instructing you in keeping with
the prophecies made earlier about you, so that by following them, you may continue to fight the good fight
with faith and a good conscience.

As I have already said, it was not my intention to publish this work. But I am a simple worker of God. I am only doing the will of the Master. I regret the fact very much that I am dragging things. Preaching is a task that I admire. I never imagined that, even in a million years, I would write a book because it is perilous. I will never forget Pastor Elysee Joseph, the late Church of God mission overseer in Haiti, who died during the earthquake of January 12, 2010. He always whispered in my ear: "We never know with God." Pastor Louis Regnel, pastor of the Church of God of,Rue Du Centre, my spiritual father, always taught me: "It would be better to say yes to God." Pastor Enock J. René, former Church of God overseer in Haiti, who pushed me to exercise my talent. And, Pastor Pierre Edner Petit-Frere of the Church of God Agape, Fort Lauderdale, Florida, whose advice filled me with hope and strength to continue the fight. My colleague, Pastor Ernst Simeus, of the Church House of Grace of Lake Worth, Florida, who helped me throughout my treacherous journey. Our collaboration gave the result that you have in your hands today. I am not saying that this work is a fin-ished work. The late President of France, François Mitterrand, said on his death bed: "Any human work is unfinished." There is still empty space to fill.

ACKNOWLEDGMENTS

First, my acknowledgments go to the Almighty who gives me the breath. I would like to thank Pastor Ernst Simeus from the depths of my heart for his advice, his persistence, his commitment to excellence, and his friendship. He had a vision of this project from the beginning and it is his belief in this project that makes me proud. I regret Pastor Marilien Madistin, my father,not live to see what his incredible support lead to.

My special thanks go to Pastor Lambert, pastor of youth to the Church of God of Rue du center, Port-au-Prince, my faithful friend.

My thanks also go to the Church of God of Mapou Lagon, of "Estere," which gave me everything. My thanks also extend to Pastor Moise Desroches of New York, Church of God of the Truth, for his wise advice. Bishop D. L. Poitier, responsible for Haitian Liaison Ministry, in Florida. Brother Assonny Joseph, Inspector to the Sunday School department of Church of God of Rue Du Centre. Me Samuel Madistin, which led me to the Church of God of Rue Du Centre, in my early childhood. I would like to be grateful to all, and to all who in one way or another have contributed to the publication of this book. By the grace of God, if I am fighting the good fight, the contributions of these brave servants of God are of paramount importance.

1

THE CHURCH

At another time in ancient Rome, a gathering of noble people met to discuss their case. It is a Greek concept: ekklēsía, (ek, "out from and to" and kaléō, "to call")[1].1577. In its essence, the Church is the community of the saints, redeemed by God, washed in the blood of Christ, born of the Spirit and heirs of salvation. By its definition, the Church does not refer to a building or a place of worship. This spiritual church is the mystical Body of Christ, giving membership by the Baptism of the Spirit. It is universal, and includes those who are dead in Christ and the living regenerated. The Church is both visible and invisible. We, the living, must unite to the faith of our predecessors (Jn17.20-21). The world must see our good works (1 Pet. 2.12). We should be fervent witnesses of God. Along with its universality, the Church is also Local: In the New Testament, the Christian community of each locality was regarded as a church, which allows you to speak "of the churches" (Acts 8.1; 11.26; 13.1; 14.23, 27; 15.41; Rom. 16.4-5; 1 Cor. 7.17; 1 Thess. 2.14). According to the scriptures, the Church was inaugurated on the day of Pentecost, the day of the bestowal of the Holy Spirit (Acts 2.1-4). The people of Israel, in the desert, represented the people of God. It is in this sense that Stephen speaks of **assembly** (Acts 7.38). Jesus uses the word **Church** for the first time in Mt. 16.18. The idea of the Church is divine, but the organization of the Church is a human institution.

---

[1] New American Standard Bible, Greek of New Testament Dictionary page 26

Milestones of the Church

According to history, the Church has experienced seven major milestones during its pilgrimage on earth.

1. The Apostolic Church (30-100AD), with the outpouring of the Holy Spirit that one associates with the church in Ephesus.
2. The Martyrs Church (100-313AD), identified with the church of Smyrna (Nero - Diocletian).
3. The Imperial Church (313-590 AD), with the ascension of the emperor Constantine that Church is identified with the church of Pergamum.
4. The Middle Ages or idolatrous or the Catholic Church (590-1517AD), that is associated with the church of Thyatira.
5. The traditional Church (1517-1648AD), that identified with the Church in Sardis.
6. The Church of the century of lights or the Church of the Reformation (1648-1789AD), that is associated with the church of Philadelphia.
7. The modern times or the Missionary Church (1789 to the present) that is identified with the church of Laodicea.

The Apostolic Church (30-303)

The New Testament is the reliable document that explains the origin of Christianity. During his earthly ministry, Jesus trained his disciples. After his resurrection, he spent forty days with his disciples to upgrade them to continue his ministry. They were told not to depart from Jerusalem, but to wait for what the Father had promised (Acts 1.4). Ten days after Jesus ascended into heaven, the apostles gathered in Jerusalem received the baptism of the Holy Spirit, by which all believers form a single body (1 Cor. 12.13). There were staying in Jerusalem many Jews, men of all nations, who had come for the feast. It should be noted that the baptism of the Holy Spirit was not yet granted before this date (Acts 1.5). The Holy Spirit spoke through Peter. He spoke of Jesus of Nazareth, whom the Romans, with the complicity of the Jews, had killed and who was risen. His speech was so persuasive and convincing that 3,000 souls were added to the number of the disciples. Since Pentecost, and only since, there is a whole that is called the Church. The date of this event is located between 28 and 33 of our era, according to the historians.

A few days later, Peter and John went to the temple to pray. They performed a miraculous healing: at the door of the Temple, they made a man walk who had been lame since birth. The apostles were responsible for many miracles. The work of the apostles was so successful in Jerusalem that every day the number of the disciples increased (Acts 2.47).

The first Christians were of one heart and one soul and one mind (Acts 4.32). They met on the first day of the week, Sunday, to pray, commune and eat together. They had everything in common (Acts 2.42, 44; 20.7).

The apostles formulated the Christian doctrine according to the authority that Jesus entrusted to them by the Holy Spirit (Jn 16.12-14; 20.21-23).

Martyrs Church (303-313)
a. **The Jewish persecution**
    The first persecution was raised by the Jewish leaders, then by the Jewish people. The Roman authorities at the beginning kept silent. Sometimes, they were called by the Jews into the path of violence[2]. These persecutions caused the expansion of the Church, which Jesus had predicted (Acts 1.8). Because of persecution, the disciples went from Jerusalem to the regions of Judea and Samaria (Acts 8.1). Shortly after, the disciples felt the need to preach the Gospel to all. Peter, because of a revelation, announced the Gospel to Cornelius (Acts 10). Other missionaries brought the Gospel to the Gentiles. For example, Barnabas was sent to Antioch by the church of Jerusalem (Acts 11), not counting the missionary voyages of Paul.

b. **The Roman persecution**
    It must be said that in ancient Rome there was the imperial cult, where the emperor was considered the equal of a god, as in ancient Babylon. It is in this sense that many think that the word **Babylon** means **Rome** (1 Pet. 5.13). The refusal of Christians to worship the emperor caused further and worse persecution by the Roman authorities. This is because the Christians, just like the Jews at the time of Daniel and his companions, would not adore anyone but the Highest God.

According to historians, Peter went to Rome in the year 61AD, and he died a martyr. The tradition tells us that because of the preaching of Peter, the four concubines of Agrippa were converted to the Lord and changed their way of life. Further, according to William Barclay, by the influence of Peter, Xanthippe, the wife of Albinus, the favorite of the emperor, was convinced

---

[2] Précis d'histoire de l'Eglise, J Marcel Nicole page 14

3

to lead a life of chastity. Agrippa and Albinus were furious and wanted Peter put to death. With extreme cruelty, they killed Peter's wife prior to killing him, and Peter was encouraged by his wife, telling him to remember the Lord. Then they crucified Peter, and at his request hung him head down, because he felt he was not worthy to die in the same way as the Master, according to William Barclay[3].

- Paul was beheaded because he was a Roman citizen (2 Tim. 4.6-8).
- Mark was dragged until death came.
- Philip was whipped, thrown in prison and then crucified.
- Bartholomew was cruelly beaten and then crucified.
- Luke was hanged on an olive tree.
- Thomas died pierced by a sword.
- Mathias was stoned and then beheaded.
- Matthew was pierced with a spear.
- James, brother of the Lord, pastor of the Church of Jerusalem, was stoned and killed with a nightstick by the Jews shortly before the destruction of Jerusalem.

The legend tells us that Andrew asked that he be crucified on an X-shaped cross because he felt he was not worthy to die on a cross like the Master, and he died at the Achaia in ancient Greece.

The Apostle John, according to history, was thrown in a pot of boiling oil, but he escaped alive. He was then sent into exile to the Island of Patmos, where he died a natural death[4].

The first official persecution began under Nero (52-68 AD), who has been accused of causing the burning of the city of Rome. To find a scapegoat, Nero accused the Christians, calling them a band of criminals who burned the city of Rome. The Christians were persecuted brutally. They knew prison, exile, and forced labor. Some were sacrificed, others sawn apart, others crucified, and others burned alive[5].

After this time of persecution, other periods of persecution began at the beginning of the second century under Trajan, Marcus Aurelius.

In 303 AD, even fiercer persecution took place, when Diocletian, pushed by its protégé Galerius, dreamed to erase Christianity. With four successive edicts, he ordered the destruction of the worship and the sacred books. He imprisoned all clerics. The faithful were forced to worship and

---

[3] William Barclay, *The Master's Men,* page 26

[4] Barclay, page 35.

[5] Nicole, page 15.

to sacrifice to idols. Some did get a certificate of convenience for having recanted, although the persecutors do not have the fact. That is what is called the lapsi (apostates). This persecution was not ended by the abdication of Diocletian, nor the death of Galerius. In 313, the triumph of Constantine brought peace to the Church. This last persecution lasted ten years, and seems to confirm the message of John (Apoc. 2.10).

Anyway, the Gospel was announced.

Imperial Church (313-1590)

In 313, Constantine issued the Edict of Milan, an edict of tolerance for the Christians. Although the emperor had not yet converted, a divine event impelled him to 8ymake this decision. On the eve of the battle at the **Milvian bridge**, against a usurper, he had a vision of the cross accompanied by an order: "**In hoc Signo Vinces**" -- "in this sign you will conquer." Therefore, he made the cross the **labarum** of his army. In recognition of the High God, he published this edict, which guaranteed freedom to Christians, and demanded that those who confiscated the assets of the Christians to return them. He made it obligatory not to work on Sunday, and reduced the powers of the unbelievers. However, he was not baptized until shortly before his death, by Eusebius.

From there, the Church became mundane, and we dealt with liberal cults:

1. Worship of images
2. The seven sacraments
   a. Baptism, administered (triple immersion or sprinkling) for adults and children forty days after birth.
   b. Confirmation immediately follows baptism.
   c. Eucharist, given with **leavened** bread and wine to all the members, including children.
   d. Penitence, a sentence imposed on the penitent to expiate his sins. It includes confession followed by absolution.
   e. Marriage.
   f. Ordination that the bishop alone can confer.
   g. Anointing with oil administered in view of healing in the event of a serious illness.
3. Purgatory

From the Catholic sect is born as the first cult that diverted from orthodoxy and not the first Church. In the third century, we had what is called the ecumenicalism of the time, the union between the State and the Church.

This church is associated with the Church of Pergamum in the book of Revelation. She had an appearance of piety and people attached to the doctrine of Balaam and of the Nicolaitans.

Church of the Middle Ages or Idolatrous Church (590-1517)

The political situation did not change in the seventh century. The Roman Empire covered the whole of the Mediterranean basin. The Germanic invasions that followed upset the political, economic, social and religious life of Europe. The kings took the habit to publish ecclesiastical laws and edicts. They also appointed bishops[6]. The bishops gathered at the councils, whose decisions were inclined to the desires of the kings. They constituted what is called a national church which, from an administrative point of view, depended on the Pope. Pope Gregory the Great even formulated the Pastoral Rule to the intention of the priests. From the point of view of doctrine, Gregory recommended the doctrine of purgatory. He consecrated its care to the liturgy, to sacred songs, to the preaching, he encouraged the use of images in the churches. It was a period of spiritual darkness. This church is identified by more than one as the church of Thyatira.

Traditional Church or the Church of the reformation (1517- 1648)

While the primitive Church had to fight against many heresies, the Church of the time of the reform had to revive the Church, which was close to death with its constituents composed of dissidents of the previous church. This is what is called the people of the second religion. This work has taken time. At the time occurred, at the peak of its power, movements of reaction appeared with Wycliffe, a professor at Oxford who stood against the immorality of the monks and the avarice of the Popes. He then stated that the Bible alone is the authority in matters of faith, rejecting the papacy and the tradition. John Hus, a professor in Prague, on reading of the works of Wycliffe, was forced to accept the Scriptures as the only authority in matters of faith. He was arrested and burned alive, in 1415, but his disciples continued the movement against the Catholic system.

In the face of the requirements of the Highest God, some saw that they could not be saved by the teachings of Catholicism. In addition, a few favorable circumstances with the appearance of the new states saw the appearance of leaders such as Martin Luther, a professor at the University of Wittenberg, who, in studying the Epistle of Paul to the Romans, realized

---

[6] Nicole, page 75

that man cannot be justified by his merits, but by grace by believing in Jesus Christ. Then after his trip to Rome, Luther wrote the 95 Theses to call for the reform of the Church. His theses were widespread and accepted, and they led to the Lutheran Reformation.

Then took place parallel and similar reforms:

a. Before 1517. Period of preparation. Lefevre of Etaples. Youth of Luther. Birth of the main reformers.
b. 1517-1523. Rupture of Luther with Rome. Zwingli in Zurich. Catholic reform of Meaux.
c. 1523-1535. Organization of Lutheranism. War of the peasants. Dissemination of the reform in Germany, Sweden, Prussia, reform in Alsace; Colloquy of Marburg. Youth of Calvin. Rupture of Henry VIII with Rome. Beginnings misfortunes of the Anabaptists.
d. 1536-1546. Reform in Denmark. Last years of Luther. The end of the reign of Henry VIII. Calvin at Geneva, in Strasbourg.
e. 1547-1558. Struggles of Calvin at Geneva. Henry II in France; Edward VI in England.
f. 1559-1569. Last Years of Calvin. Organization of the Reformed Churches of France. Calvinist reform in Hungary, Poland, Scotland, in some German states.

At the start of the reformation all the Protestant churches were unanimous that the Bible was the only authority in matters of faith and that salvation was free. The ecclesiastical organization and the relationship with the states being different on the forms of worship. This Church is like the church of Sardis, in which the spiritual life was lacking, and despite everything had a few men of distinction[7].

Church of the century of Lights or the Church of the reformation (1648-1789)

After the Reformation which had shaken the Church of Rome (emperor) and the political, economic, social and cultural life of Europe, according to historians, the western waters were already boiling. The truth of the Gospel message would continue to make waves.

The Reformation broke free the concepts known and received until then. This bomb removed the veil of the darkness of ignorance, superstition, error, and spiritual and intellectual slavery.

---

[7] Nicole, page 159

This upheaval of the whole society was done in a framework, without being a war of religion.

The political, economic, social, and especially the intellectual and spiritual explosions facilitated the movements of awakenings. People acquired new knowledge. Is this not the fulfilment in part of the prophecy of Daniel, when he said in Dan. 12.4: you, Daniel, shut up the words, and seal the book until the time of the end; many shall run to and fro, and knowledge shall increase. The revolution of the 16th century wanted a Gospel in the love, conviction, grace, clarity, and power of God, rooted in the New Testament. And this message has served as a guide to lead the whole of Europe toward new horizons. The spirit of man has been released by the assurance of salvation. There have been alarm clocks with valiant heroes of the faith, such as:

a. John Wesley was converted on 24 May 1738 in listening of the reading "The preface of the Epistle to the Romans," written by Luther, and who brought together sometimes 20,000 members to its audience.

b. Pastor Jonathan Edwards (1703-1758). A rigid Calvinist. He divided his sermons into two parts, exposure and application, and read without the change of volume of voice, without gesture, without any effort of rhetoric, but with a depth of conviction. The Church of the century of lights and alarm clocks has been identified as the Church of Philadelphia

Church of the Modern Time or Missionary Church (1789 to present)

From the primitive Church, up until the Middle Ages, the Church was separated from the world in which it evolved. Its limits were spiritual. After the Middle Ages, it would seem to identify with the Christianized. Even after the Reform, this design was maintained up to the end of the eighteenth century. The links between the Church and the nominally Christian states, very strong until then, have been released and sometimes broken in our days. In 1787, the Constitution of the United States excluded the existence of a Church state.

Among other things, the end of the eighteenth century and the beginning of the nineteenth century have been marked by rationalism and indifference. Missionary societies were beginning to form.

In 1792, William Carey of England founded the Missionary Society of India, an organized movement for the evangelism of the pagan world. The

Methodists revival, with the disciples of Wesley, took over more land. In 1923, we have had revivals in the Reformed churches.

While this Church, heir to a richness and a power, became mechanized, proud. We had different philosophies and views in the CHURCH. The Church lost its beauty, purity of doctrine, and prestige. More and more the CHURCH looks like the Church of Laodicea as it is described by John:" ... You are neither cold nor hot" (Revelation 3.15)

The CHURCH has fallen into the apostasy spoken by Paul. The Church ceases to operate. But good hope, Jesus said:" I will build my Church, and the gates of Hades shall not prevail against it" (Matthew 16.18). Paul had well said that the advent of Christ would not happen before the apostasy (2 Thessalonians 2.3).

Anyone who has ears should listen!

2

THE CHURCH
AND THE WORLD

1. The Church and the Social Action

According to the dichotomous theory, the human being is composed of a material part and an immaterial part. The Church must not evolve only on spiritual plans, but also must participate in social development. It is not necessary for the Church to invest only in missionary programs, but must also be involved in social programs such as: charitable works, school and university education, development organizations, emergency services, the fight against AIDS, water and sanitary facilities, irrigation, urbanization, etc.

At this point, it should be noted the action of the Prophet Elisha concerning the city of Jericho, when he restored the waters of Jericho. Was this not a social action? The reproaches of Jesus to the goats in Matthew 25.41-43, "I was hungry, and you did not feed me. I was thirsty, and you did not give me a drink. I was a stranger, and you did not invite me into your home. I was naked, and you did not give me clothing. I was sick and in prison, you did not visit me", are aimed at different social works.

The apostle James said in Jas 2.24, "a man is justified by works and not by faith alone." If we love people to salvation, we must do what we are able.

The Church must pursue its objectives. The importance attached to social issues in our current time means the Church of the third millennium must undertake social actions. Jesus said: "... but these are in this world."

(Jn17.11b) So, the Church's mission is always to undertake social actions. But for the work to be more effective, it must be organized. The Church must have a mode of life as in the past. In the past God chose the nation of Israel and put in the middle of it three categories of leaders to help the people in their pilgrimage: the priests, the prophets and the kings, with their respective roles. The priests were responsible to present the sacrifice of the people to God. The prophets were responsible to carry the messages of God to the people, while the kings were responsible for social affairs. We must note that the first two categories were employed in the spiritual field and the last in the social field. So, we did not need only spiritual programs but also social programs to the extent that the latter do not impede the spiritual life. It is a privilege that God has given us, to transmit his love where we live: in our villages, our cities, our place of work, our entire society. Let us accept this privilege.

2. The Church and Culture

Definition of Culture
Culture, in the large sense, is the set of all distinctive traits, spiritual and material, intellectual and effective, which characterize a society. It also encompasses the arts and letters, the modes of life, the fundamental rights of the human being, value systems, traditions and beliefs.

There are two kinds of culture

a.   culture on the individual plan: all acquired by instruction, the knowledge of a human being.
b.   culture on the collective plan such as intellectual, artistic, etc. achievements that characterize a society.

In this sense, it is said: culture is a social transmission.

Christian Doctrine

It is the fundamental point of the Christian faith. Any ecumenical movement that does not disturb Christian doctrine is permitted to any Christian. Customs and practices vary from one country to another. Christians need a code of ethics to differentiate themselves in the middle of the world, a mode of life to please God, to build up other Christians, and maintain the salvation of the pagan. Therefore, Christians must make sure of what they do, what they say, and where they go. The apostle Paul exhorts us in this sense:" for if we live, we live for the Lord; and if we die, we die to the Lord.

Therefore, whether we live or die, we are the Lord's. "(Rom. 14.8). The Christian must avoid any secret movement: "we have renounced secret and shameful ways; we do not use deception, nor do we distort the word of God. On the contrary, by setting forth the truth plainly we commend ourselves to everyone's conscience in the sight of God "(2 Cor. 4.2) Christians must be proud of their participation in a cultural movement, and must have an irreproachable conscience:" Then those who heard it, being convicted by their conscience, went out one by one, beginning with the oldest even to the last" (Jn 8.9a).

The apostle Paul made a note to the Philippians in this sense: "Finally, brethren, whatever things are true, whatever things are noble, whatever things are just, whatever things are just, whatever things are pure, whatever things are lovely, whatever things are of good report, if there is any virtue and if there is anything praiseworthy -- meditate on these things" (Phil. 4.8). To the Corinthians Paul had said:" All things are lawful for me, but all things are not helpful. All things are lawful for me, but I will not be brought under the power of any" (1 Cor. 6.12). There are still a few points to exhaust before we close this series.

The manner of dress varies from one people to another, according to the climate, the eras, the tastes and the religion. The Christian must be neither outmoded or overtaken by the social fashion. Christians can attach to a social fashion if it does not offend God. They must dress with simplicity. They do not have to comply with the social fashion of the current times: "Do not conform to the pattern of this world, but be transformed by the renewing of your mind. Then we will be able to test and approve what God's will is -- his good, pleasing and perfect will" (Rom. 12.2).

Religious dance is a way for Christians to manifest their joy before God for his benefits:" He jumped to his feet and began to walk. Then he went with them into the temple, walking and jumping, and praising God" (Acts 3.8). It is recommended to the people of God:" let them praise his name with the dance; let them sing praise to him with the tumbrel and harp" (Ps 149.3). The religious dance is a gesture of humility before God. King David danced before the Lord during the transportation of the Ark to Jerusalem: "And I will be yet more vile than this, and will be base in mine own sight: but of the handmaids of whom thou hast spoken, of them shall I be had in honor" (2 Sam. 6.22). This dance was not done in the darkness, since Michal could see from a distance. It was not with two different sexes, in a sense unclean, because it had not energized the jealousy of Michal, but in a sense of praise and worship. However, Satan masquerades as an angel of light to pervert everything that is sacred: "And this is not surprising since Satan disguises himself as an angel of light" (2 Cor. 11.14).

Dance, according to the world: a rapprochement of the sexes under the influence of music.

Sometimes dances are accompanied by drink to excite carnal passions. The dance, according the world's standards, leads to immorality. Dancing in the court of King Herod cost the life of John the Baptist:" But when Herod's birthday was celebrated, the daughter of Herodias danced before them and pleased Herod. Therefore, he promised with an oath to give her whatever she might ask. So, she, having been prompted by her mother, said, Give me John the Baptist's head here on a platter" (Mt. 14.6-8).

We must pay attention to what we are doing. The joy of this world is temporary, but the joy of God is eternal. My dear companions, we are fighting heroically and we will see the glory of God.

3. The Christian and the Politic

Several leaders of the past have banned the politic in the Christian environment, because at their time it was common to the Church. Those leaders of the past had not shown the ambiguity of the term!

The politic, what is it? Is it the conflict of persons and petty interests? Or made of hypocrisy and lies?

The **honorable Senator Samuel Madistin** has defined in his book, the politic in the following way:

> The concept "political" derived from the Greek word "polis" which means city-states." the city or the "polis" was in the eyes of the Greeks the unit by excellence of social life, the optimum grouping of human beings. The legislator continues to say that the Greek political thinking conceived the "polis" as moral association to live in common according to the good and for the good.[8]

From the point of view of the Bible: The Prophet Elisha spoke to Jehoram, the king of Israel, with a notorious impertinence: Elisha said to the king of Israel:" What have I to do with you? Go to the prophets of your father and the prophets of your mother" (2 Kings 3.13).

Elijah the prophet spoke to King Ahab, whose corrupt life was a shame for Israel: "Have you murdered and taken possession?" (1 Kings 21.19). Moses went in front of Pharaoh. In the New Testament, Jesus spoke of

---

[8] Samuel Madistin, *The Role of Legislative Power in The Modern Operation of the State, page 27*

Herod, who did not manifest a great respect for him (politician formed in Rome): "...Go, tell that fox..." (Lk. 13.32).

Closer to us, Martin Luther was politically incorrect for having resisted the religious power and especially the policy of the Pope. He brought about the great awakening of the Reformation, which we enjoy even today, by the grace of God.

In my humble opinion, the politic taken in its etymological sense is not something unclean. I am not talking about the faults. Do not forget as a Christian, for any business, we need God with us: "and whatever you do, in word or deed, do everything in the name of the Lord Jesus, giving thanks to God the Father through him" (Col. 3.17).

What about the positions? Can a pastor be president of a country or a member of the government?

The government, according to Senator Madistin, is the holder of political power. It exercises effective authority exclusive over the territory and the population.[9]

The Apostle Paul tells us that the magistrate is the servant of God for your good (Rom. 13.4). What is a magistrate?

According to the Hachette Dictionary: the magistrate: official or civil officer invested with a jurisdictional authority, political or administrative.

Dahrendorf defines the authority: "probability that an order with a certain specific content will result in the obedience of a given group of persons." Authority exists in any human community; in the groups of prayers, songs, study etc[10]. My brothers and sisters in the LORD, do not add and do not subtract from the Word of God.

4. The Christian and the Army

When I say the army, I include the police, because they have the same characteristics. What does the New Testament say on this subject?

When John was baptizing, there were members of the military who asked him what they should do to have life. John answered: "Do not extort money and do not accuse people falsely. And be content with your pay" (Lk. 3.14). These three characteristics are often located among military personnel. Otherwise, they could keep their positions.

The Roman centurion, Cornelius, was a leader of a large military unit who exercised piety. He practiced the piety well toward his entourage. Peter had not required him to resign to his position to please God.

---

[9] Madistin, page 32

[10] Madistin, page 28

The question is how to seek the will of God in all that you undertake, because Isaiah said: "Woe to the rebellious children, says the Lord, who take counsel, but not of me...." (Isa. 30.1). Then we need the light of the sky on our path.

5. The Christian and the Carnival

Carnival is a festival whose origin remains unknown.

> Daniel Fabre in his book, *The Carnival or the Feast Upside Down,* associated the success of Babylon to the Roman Saturnalia and the Jewish festival of Purim. In the sixth century AD, the Persians invaded Babylon, and according to James G. Frater they would have been the instigators of the carnival.

The etymological origin of the carnival is no less controversial and obscure. Some theories escalate this etymology to "Carrus Navalis," i.e., "naval chariot" who took part in the Roman feast of Isis (Egyptian goddess adopted by the Romans and the Greeks).

According to the *Historical Dictionary of the French Language*, the most likely cause is that of the Latin word "carnelevare" (XS), composed of "carne" (meat) and "levare" (leave, lift), which means abstain from meat; by the thirteenth century, we already know the Italian word "Carnevalo," where we get the current word carnival. Less ambiguous is the Portuguese word, "Entrudo," and the Galician "Entroido" came from the Latin "introit," which means to enter Lent and, by metonymy, the time that precedes Lent, i.e., the carnival.

Despite the lack of light on its etymological origin, the carnival remains a period of variable time, according to the use of the country and the regions or the people, for practices contrary to the established social order, or unhealthy. Under the cover of a mask, almost everything is allowed and justified. In fact, the mask and disguise, being the essential elements of the carnival, liberate participants from the daily tensions, which explains the high tolerance of the authorities. So, it is not suitable for a Christian.

The Apostle Paul said:" Finally, brethren, whatever things are true, whatever things are noble, whatever things are just, whatever things are just, whatever things are pure, whatever things are lovely, whatever things are of good report, if there is any virtue and if there is anything praiseworthy -- meditate on these things" (Philippians 4.8). The carnival is an unhealthy and unclean place, and it may not be the subject of thoughts for Christians.

By contrast, the exercise of your profession or your work can lead you to this place, but not as a participant or actor. Flee the dark road of misleading pleasure, and you will have the joy of God.

We are in this world!

3

THE DIRECTION OF
THE CHURCH

A leader is someone who knows the way, goes the way, and shows the way. [11]

Jesus said: "... if the blind lead the blind, both will fall into a pit" (Mt. 15.14). From this point, the idea of leadership involves people who lead others. So, if you are leaders, it must necessarily be that there are people who follow you. A shepherd without sheep is not a shepherd.

The terms shepherds and sheep are very critical. The sheep are animals which, by their enormous weakness, cannot operate without a shepherd. The sheep are animals of value, as Christ explained in the parable of the goats and sheep in the book of Matthew. The value of the sheep is so large that even the angels of God rejoice for a lost sheep which was found. The importance of the sheep is such that in ancient Rome, the law prohibited shooting sheep. The sheep lived in groups, and the law of ancient Rome said that sheep are so related that if someone withholds a sheep in his field in violation, it may require the cost of liberation by counting all the sheep of the flock. Spiritual leaders like the shepherds are different from secular leaders. Jesus himself said in Mt. 20.25-26, "the rulers of the Gentiles lord it over them, and those who are great exercise authority over them. Yet it shall not be so among you; but whoever desires to become great among you, let him be your servant." The spiritual leaders are servants, giving examples of love to the people.

Leaders are necessary to the Church because there will always be problems to solve. This was the case in the primitive Church and in the

---

[11] Tony Evans, *God's Glorious CHURCH*, page 127

ages of the Church. And even in the tribes of Israel. The organization of the Church is necessary for a better job. The church of the assembly of Israel in the desert provides the example of Moses and the seventy elders. On the advice of Jethro, his father-in-law who was a priest in Midian, Moses had made the distribution of tasks. Then closer to us, Jesus chose twelve men he had prepared to be with him in the work." Though Jesus himself did not baptize, but his disciples" (Jn 4.2).

It is important for us to reconsider the elements of history that will help us to better direct the Church of Jesus Christ by the means of the Holy Spirit.

We need a distribution of tasks, because the task is immense, and hard is the field. Jesus and Paul were not too concerned about the question of baptism. To repeat the words of Paul to the Corinthians:" For Christ did not send me to baptize..." (1 Cor. 1.17). Peter and the apostles were not too concerned with the question of the distribution of food; "it is not desirable that we should leave the Word of God and serve tables" (Acts 1.2). Therefore, a single man is not enough for the work of God. Regarding the model to adopt, this will depend on the choice, the capacity of the Church, but it must be a distribution of tasks.

Deacons and the Administration
A. The deacons

The word deacon comes from the Greek diakonos, which means servant.
The deacon is a Christian carrying an auxiliary function in the local church.

1. **Qualifications**
To be a deacon, there must be: (according to Acts 6.3)
   a. Have a good testimony - honorable.
   b. Be full of the Holy Spirit - spiritual.
   c. Be full of wisdom - practice.

2. **Responsibilities**
   a. They must pray for the church and the members.
   b. They must monitor the concerns of the members.
   c. They must visit the members of the church.
   d. They must help the pastor to keep the discipline of the church.
   e. They must cooperate in the decisions taken by the pastor for the good operation of the church.
   f. They must know the rights and duties of states.

3. **Choice**

The choice can be done in two ways:

a. Election or designation.

Designation comes from the Greek "cheirotone," which means "vote by raising the hand." This is the term that is used by Paul in Acts 14.23 "...they had ordained them elders in every church..."

b. Appointment

In Titus 1:5, the Apostle Paul said that he left Titus in Crete, that he put in order what remained to be adjusted, and that he establishes elders in each city. The word "establish" of the Greek "kathistemi," means "secure, place, install, load someone of something" or "entrust to someone the administration of a function." Therefore, this passage deals with the idea of appointment.

4. **Internal Regulation of the Body**

a. Obligation for the deacons to present themselves to the meetings (a kind of penalty should be laid down for several unexcused absences).

b. Obligation to the deacons to give information on their work.

c. Deacons may be attached to the administration.

d. The information discussed in the meetings must be confidential even for their families.

5. **The Term of Their Mandate**

The duration of their mandate depends on the administration of the church for the good conduct of the work of God.

B. The Administration

1. The administration must have at least a deacon.
2. Persons working in the administration of the church must properly manage the property of the church with all its contents.
3. If there are laws relating, they must adhere to them.
4. The directors must be Christians and have authority in the management of business.
5. The administration may recommend salaries for some personnel of the church.
6. If there is no finance committee, the administration oversees the finances.

7. The term of the administration depends on the laws and conditions of the church.
8. All the information discussed by the administration must be confidential.

For a better spread of the Gospel, it is necessary that the Church is distributed in departments according to its size

1. Sunday School Department
2. Music Department
3. Evangelism Department
4. Women's Department
5. Men's Department
6. Youth Department
7. Social Affairs Department
8. Finance Department
9. Children Department

There are not only departments, there is also the necessary work concerning the pastoral ministry such as:

a. The pastor and the members
b. The pastor and the child consecration
c. The pastor and the business meeting
d. The pastor and the ordinances
e. The pastor and home visitation
f. The pastor and the Holy Communion service
g. Church planting
h. The pastor-advisor

Paul said in Phil. 4.8, "Finally, brethren, whatever things are true, whatever things are noble, whatever things are just, whatever things are just, whatever things are pure, whatever things are lovely, whatever things are of good report, if there is any virtue and if there is anything praiseworthy -- meditate on these things." The creation of these departments was not in the Bible, but it is the subject of our thoughts as well, so we will show them to you.

We are working better and better to the work of the Lord!

4

SUNDAY SCHOOL DEPARTMENT

1. History of the Sunday school

I n the fourth century AD, Gregory the artist began very fruitful Bible schools for children in Armenia. In 680 AD, the Fifth Council of Constantinople recommended the creation of schools in the churches, with the Bible as the manual of reference. The importance of the school was noted by the leaders of the Reform, such as Luther, Zwingli, Knox and Calvin[12].

Robert Raikes, philanthropist and editor in England, organized the Sunday school in the form of schools. In 1780, he began his experience in the kitchen of Madam Meredith. Its first students came from the lowest classes of society and were known as rowdy and offenders. Robert Raikes focused on these children, aged six to fourteen years, who gathered around him each Sunday from 10:00 AM to noon and 2:00 PM to 5:00 PM for the study of the Word of God. After having established several schools in different bottom neighborhoods of Gloucester (England) and after rich experiences, R. Raikes decided to make public the movement on November 3, 1783.[13]

After the death of Raikes, in 1811, the Sunday schools of England had approximately 400,000 students. The Raikes' movement moved to the United States of America in 1785 with William Elliot, who founded

---

[12] Stephen Rexroat ,*Sunday School Spirit*, page 12

[13] Rexroat, page 15

a Sunday school for his slaves, an activity imitated by other slave masters. The Methodist Church of the United States also began in the circuit in 1790.[14]

At the beginning of the twentieth century, the United States had nearly 20,000,000 pupils in Sunday schools.

In some environments, the Sunday school has no structure of home or human resources to develop. However, it made an impeccable work, which has enabled the lamp of the Lord to stay lit.

2. The Mission of the Sunday School
   a. Win souls to Christ.
   b. Teach the Word of God.
   c. Build Christian character by teaching.
   d. Provide spiritual assistance to believers.
   e. Engage the believers in service.
   f. Work for the spiritual growth of the believer.
   g. Help students to integrate within the church.
   h. Guide the teaching body in a suitable direction.
   i. Equip leaders with helpful advice.
   j. Prepare leaders with the goal of serving better.

3. Role of the Pastor or Officer Responsible
   a. Must do his best to identify gaps and any embarrassing element for the good functioning of the institution.
   b. Responsible for the program of the Sunday school: seminars, training, conferences, reflection, and symposia for the Sunday school teachers.
   c. Responsible for the recruitment of the Sunday school teachers.
   d. Must ensure the application of the principles of the Sunday school or the statutes of the Sunday school.
   e. Must serve as an intermediary between the faculty and the church.
   f. Presides over the meetings of the steering committee.

4. Composition of the Steering Committee
   a. Pastor responsible
   b. Secretary General
   c. Deputy Secretary General
   d. Treasurer
   e. Assistant Treasurer

---

[14] Rexroat, page 21

f. Prefects of discipline
g. Advisors
h. Inspectors
i. Delegates

5. Role of the Secretary General

a. Represents the teaching body with the approval of the pastor.
b. Presides over the meetings of the steering committee in case of the absence of the pastor.
c. Prepares the minutes of the meetings of the steering committee
d. Presents the report of the activities of the teaching body to the general assemblies of the Sunday school teaching body.
e. Stimulates the students regarding numbers, donations, and the Bibles.
f. Presents a general report every Sunday to the church on the activities of the classes from the reports from the different sections.
g. Makes a summary of the Sunday lesson to the church to encourage the believers and the participants to put into practice the moral teachings and spiritual needs of the lesson presented by the teachers.
h. Ensures the timely availability of books for the Sunday lesson
i. Ensures that all the Sunday school teachers regularly participate in the preparatory course in the Sunday lesson.
j. Holds the registry to control the presence of monitors at preparatory courses for the Sunday lesson.
k. Holds the archives of the body

6. Role of the Deputy Secretary General

The Deputy Secretary General plays the same role as the Secretary General and is empowered to replace him or her in the case where the latter would be absent.

7. Role of the Treasurer

a. Keeps the treasury of the Sunday School body
b. Receives the contributions of the church
c. Prepares and submits an annual financial report on the management of receipts and disbursement of funds of the teaching body to the general assemblies of the teaching body.
d. Submits a quarterly balance sheet detailing the activities of the teachers in the administration of the church, copying to the pastor responsible for the Sunday school.

8. The Role of the Assistant Treasurer

The assistant treasurer plays the same role as the treasurer and is empowered to replace him or her in case of absence.

9. Role of Prefects of Discipline

a. Monitors good behavior and the morality of the teachers.
b. Ensures the maintenance of order and discipline of the teaching body

10. Role of Advisors

Advisors provide the Sunday school their good guidance.

a. Follows the general evolution of the teaching body and considers the moral behavior and spiritual development of teachers and of all students.
b. Provides the leaders of the Sunday school all the timely advice necessary to improve the smooth running of the teaching body.

11. Role of Inspectors

Inspectors will assume the task of supervising the coordination of the activities of the teaching body and following the evolution and functioning of classes at the time of the teaching of the Sunday lesson.

12. Role of Delegates

a. To ensure communication between the secretary general of the Sunday school and the entities of the local church and all other institutions and personalities.
b. Ensures the purchase of teaching materials.

13. Role of the Secretaries of Sections

The secretaries of sections coordinate the activities of sections each in relation to it. They prepare the reports and the route to the secretary general to present to the church every Sunday after the presentation of the lesson.

14. Creation of Commissions

In support with the secretary general of the department, the pastor may appoint commissions of:

a. Recreation and maintenance
b. Devotion
c. Home visitation

d. Education and training
e. Mediation and public relations

15. Duties of Commissions
a. Recreation and Maintenance Commission

1. Organize recreational moments for the benefit of the members of the teaching body: travel (tours), camp, visiting historical sites, recreational days etc.
2. Prepare the Sunday meal
3. Organize the feasts of the Sunday school

b. Devotional Commission

1. Coordinate the devotional spiritual activities and of the department
2. Manage the spiritual services placed under the responsibility of the teacher corps
3. Ensure the devotional part at the beginning and at the end of Sunday school and the hours of preparation of the lesson.

c. Visitation Commission

1. Promote hospitality visits organized by members of the teaching body.
2. Direct visitors to the appropriate classes
3. Encourage the teachers in the organization of the visits.

d. Education and Training Commission
1. Ensure the biblical training of the members of the body
2. Organize conferences, seminars, reflections of biblical studies, roundtables and symposia and everything that can contribute to improving the benefits for teachers.
3. Promote literary and social clubs to encourage biblical character.
4. Encourage the teachers to improve their biblical and intellectual formation.

e. Mediation and Public Relations Commission
1. Ensure communication between the Sunday School Department and other entities of the church.
2. Publish all the new provisions taken by the steering committee.

3. Communicate to the members of the teaching body any informa-tion concerning them. (by notice, circular, memorandum...)
4. Serve as an intermediary between the teachers and the General Secretariat of the Sunday School.

16. Qualifications of the General Secretary

1. Be a baptized member since.........
2. Be a person of prayer, faith, vision and have a behavior worthy of the Gospel.
3. Have adequate biblical and intellectual knowledge
4. Can keep the archives of the body.
5. Can plan, in concert with the pastor, the program of the depart-ment and coordinate all activities relating thereto, to find literary resources, important religious documents, to identify the needs, to propose the elements of a solution, and to settle all details concerning the supervision and the placement of the monitors.
6. Have the capacity to develop training projects designed to increase the effectiveness of the teachers, and extend the department of biblical teaching to include all the believers of the church.
7. Can prepare in collaboration with the education and training committee a program intended to teach the teachers to speak in public.

17. The Duties

Once elected or appointed, the leader must:

a. Work on the development of the Sunday school
b. Develop plans and implement them in concert with the other offi-cials of the Sunday school.

18. Qualifications of the Treasurer

a. Be a baptized member since.........
b. Be devoted to the Lord
c. Have accounting knowledge
d. Be disciplined in the management of funds.

19. Qualifications of the Prefects of Discipline, Advisors, Inspectors, Delegates and Secretaries of Sections

a. The prefect of discipline must:
    - - Be a member.

- - Enjoy a good testimony in the church and elsewhere.
- - Be suitable, welcoming and friendly.

b. Advisors must:
   - - Be a member since ... and have teaching experience
   - - Enjoy a good testimony in the church and elsewhere
   - - Have a Christian life rich in spiritual experiences
c. An inspector must:
   - - Be a member and have teaching experience
   - - Enjoy a good testimony in the church and elsewhere
   - - Be an active leader in the exercise of its position
d. A delegate must:
   - - Be a member and have teaching experience
   - - Enjoy a good testimony in the church and elsewhere
   - - Have a Christian life rich in spiritual experiences
e. The secretary of a section must:
   - - Be a member and have teaching experience
   - - Enjoy a good testimony in the church and elsewhere
   - - can write and to keep the reports of the section

20. Choosing Candidates to Fill Positions

The choosing can be done in two ways:

a. By appointment
b. By election

All methods can bring success or failure. The difference is that by the elective voice, the burden of failure is shared among the voters. But in much of cases where the church is not too well equipped, filling positions of responsibility is usually by appointment. This section is treated with much more care in the choice of the deacons in the previous chapter.

21. The distribution of classes considering the numbers of student and the means available, in some cases:

a. Children: 0-7 years
b. Cadets: 8-13 years
c. Juniors: 14-17 years
d. Young people: 18-29 years
e. Adults: 30-x years

Note: Children must be organized by considering the habit of children to play.

For young people, this age commonly called the age of puberty is a very difficult period to handle and presents problems. In the great majority of cases, consider:

    a. Spiritual problems
    b. Social problems
    c. Emotional problems
    d. Moral problems

For the adults:
    In most cases, at the beginning they think that the Sunday school will bring nothing to them. Remember that you can use their experiences in the discussions in the class.
    In other cases, the classes are mixed:
    In cases where young people and adults would be mixed, there must be a suitable method to enable the two groups to benefit from the advantages of the Sunday school.

22. The teachers

They must be chosen with care because the task is great in the eyes of God. The one who is faithful in the small things, God will entrust him with very much.

A teacher must:

    -   Not be a new convert
    -   Be disciplined
    -   Have a minimum intellectual knowledge
    -   Be consecrated
    -   Be passionate about the study of the Word of God
    -   Be interested in his work of teaching

23. The Task of the teacher:

    -   Show students the plans of God.
    -   Form the character of students to what they see in Christ their Savior and their Master.
    -   Keep well all responsibilities with respect to students.
    -   Create opportunities for students.
    -   Keep the class orderly.

24. The Funds of the Sunday School

    a.   The budget of the Sunday school must be studied and prepared by those responsible for the body, in collaboration with the general secretary, to be then submitted to the pastor and the church for approval.

    b.   Management of the funds

The allocation of the administration of the church granted to the treasurer of the body must be managed in collaboration with those responsible for the body. All transactions must be recorded.

This book of the law shall not depart out of thy mouth!

5

MUSIC AND SERVICE DEPARTMENT

Someone said: "Music is a universal language that everyone understands." When you talk about this language, this helps the transition between an old and a new generation which has need to stand up and take its place in history. The music in the divine service is for the good of the church. It often is very far from the objective. Sometimes the music does not have the desired effect on those who listen. The music should be beautiful, powerful and touching.

The Psalms were at the heart of the Jewish liturgy in synagogue worship and the temple. Music had a privileged place in Christian worship from the beginning. During the whole of the Middle Ages and the centuries that followed, the greatest geniuses of music have created works that have incorporated the life of the Christian church. We are therefore going to introduce you to a prescription for musical harmony in Christian services.

The Subdivisions of the Department of Music

A. Music and Worship

Those who share their musical talents should do so for God. The glory of the Lord, rather than selfish gain, should be the motivation of these people.

There are certain characteristics that the members of the committee of music, musicians, soloists, the members of choirs and the leaders of the service must have:

1. Each must be Christian in the faith and in practice.
2. Each must have a practical knowledge of church music.
3. Everyone must be able to take constructive criticism.

4. Each must have a pleasant personality.
5. Each must have a humble spirit in the aim to give all the glory to God.
6. Each must be voluntary, to cooperate with each other.
7. Each must have a sense of humor.
8. Each must have the ability to encourage the other.
9. Each must be punctual in arriving.

B. The Purpose of Church Music

1. To provide a source of blessing and comfort to Christians
2. To give a medium of service to the participants: congregation and chorale
3. To provide doctrinal instruction
4. To give an expression of worship and praise
5. To give a means to unite the congregation
6. To offer an invitation to the unsaved
7. To provide a means to attract people to the church
8. To stimulate attention and interest.

C. Personnel and Procedures of the Music of the Church

1. **The Music Committee:**
   a. Serves as a liaison between the pastor and the congregation, the pastor and other committees, the pastor, and deacons.
   b. Serves as an administrator for music programs:
      - Planning (revivals, concerts, the Crusades)
      - Promotions for the evangelical groups.
      - Supervision of groups and choirs.
      - Management of instruments, purchases, rankings, controlling the PA system,

2. **The Accompanist:**
   a. Must have a practical knowledge of Christian music.
   b. Must plan and practice often.
   c. Must be in a position where he can see the leader when he plays.
   d. Must follow the leader of songs.
   e. Must lead on his/her instrument if there is no officer of singing.
   f. Introductions must establish the timing and the mood of the song.
   g. Introductions must finish on the same note with which the song began.

31

    h.   Must give much time for good breathing between the stanzas.
    i.   Must not neglect the melody of the song at any time.
    j.   Must be certain that the volume of the accompaniment is regulated in view of the dimensions of the group and the acoustics of the room.
    k.   Must play high enough to give adequate support to the soloist.
    l.   Must follow a soloist, rather than try to lead.

3. **The Choir Director**
   a. Must have the ability to lead.
   b. Must be able to encourage others.
   c. Must be able to control the choir at any time.
   d. Must make sure his directions can be seen by everyone in the choir and orchestra.
   e. Must not be focused too much on the audience.
   f. Must be able to read music and have some ability to play the piano.

4. **The Choir Members**
   a. Must have strong voices.
   b. Must be cooperative and willing to work.
   c. Must have the desire to follow the director.
   d. Must sing without calling attention to themselves.

5. **The Leader of Songs**
   1. Must make a good appearance.
   2. Must have a good voice.
   3. Must be friendly.
   4. Must know the church hymns well.
   5. Must choose hymns with these principles in the thought:
      1. Intrinsic Value
      2. Suitable Music
      3. Condensability of songs
   6. Must know in advance if a hymn is new to the congregation.
   7. Must be in a place where he can see the whole congregation.
   8. Should plan the number of stanzas to sing.
   9. Must avoid folding the song book.
   10. Must say which BOOK the song is coming from, as well as the song number.
   11. Must be aware of the length of the introduction of each hymn.
   12. Must tell the congregation when it must stand.

13. Must avoid the competitions of songs among the pews.
14. Must lead the audience, instead of following it.
15. Must praise, and not scold.
16. Should not judge the quality of the song based on its volume.
17. Must keep smiling even in errors.
18. Must finish the song service before enthusiasm dies out.

D. The Pastor and the Music of the Church
1. Must be interested in music.
2. Must plan the music program.
3. Must give constructive criticism.
4. Must help to recruit new members of the choirs.
5. Must encourage the choirs in prayer.

E. Evaluation of Music of the Church
1. How to evaluate a song.
   - Is it well said?
   - Does the song speak of God or of man?
   - Is it the best song that can be found on this subject?
   - Is it sentimental, emotional or puerile?
   - Is it beautiful poetry?

2. How to evaluate the song to sing
   - Is singing considered only as a part of the preliminary?
   - Is the song poorly used to generate feeling and enthusiasm?
   - Is it meant to be spectacular?
   - Is there a balance in the selection of songs?

F. Planning the Music of the Church
1. Songs of services
   a. The songs of services of Sunday morning must be more songs of adoration, a type of songs centered on God, the Trinity, the church and prayer.
   b. The songs of evening service must be more songs of praise, of testimony and inspiration.
   c. The songs must be chosen to coincide with the theme of the service.
   d. The songs must be chosen to mark the different step of the service.
      1) Adoration, example: *Oh Happy Day* ...

2) Praise, example: The name of Jesus is so sweet...
3) Testimony, example: *Because he loved me so...*
4) Prayer, example: My Jesus, I love thee...
5) Confession, example: *All to Jesus I surrender...*
6) Invitation, example: Just as I am, without one plea...
7) Benediction, example: Abide with me...

2. Choir
   - Prepare plans
   - Insist on the necessity of practice for members
   - Check the plans a little before the performance
   - Explain to the soloist what is desired
   - Check the means of transportation of members
   - Write a note of appreciation for the service rendered

G. Singing Aids

   - Song sheets for the songs and the choruses that are not in the books.
   - "Songs that help" on Sunday evening; songs that are sung by memory while the lights are diminished. Choose the songs in the same suit.
   - Choose a time for learning songs.
   - Types of songs to sing:

1. The stories in song.
2. The songs of the season: Easter, Pentecost, harvest, Christmas.
3. Songs by living authors.
4. Songs by old authors or composers.
5. Songs by authors who wrote both the words and the music.
6. Variation in singing:
   a. Sing a stanza if the stave is suitable.
   b. Allow the accompanist to change the key before the congregation finishes singing the last stanza. Be sure to alert the congregation of the change.
   c. Repeat a stanza in unison.

H. Order of Service

1. The service
    a. Worship begins as you enter in the sanctuary. Find your place, bow your head or kneel in prayer. This is the prelude to the service.
    b. Pray for your church, your world, those you love and yourself.
    c. Keep complete silence when the musicians give the prelude of the service.
    d. Before the service, talk to God. During the service, let God speak to you. After the service, talk to one another.

2. Call to Worship
    a. Greeting
        - -The leader
        - -The congregation
    b. Motivation
        - -Joy to be in the presence of God
        - -Gratitude
    c. Commitment
        - -Citation of an appropriate portion of Scripture
        - -Canticle
        Example:
        Brothers and sisters in Jesus Christ, I greet you all in the precious name of our divine Savior Jesus Christ. that his grace and his peace you share again! The Psalmist said in Psalm 118.1, OH, give thanks to the Lord, for he is good! For his mercy endures forever. For this, we ask the assistance to stand to demonstrate our cries of joy and gratitude to the Lord! With the canticle...

3. The announcements
    a. Other services /activities of the week.
    b. Requests for prayers (names).
    c. Next week.
    d. Thanks.
    e. Welcoming of new members.

SUPPLEMENT TO SERVICE

INVOCATION PRAYER

It is a short prayer asking for the help of God and recommends the assembly to God. The presence of God and his blessing are invoked on the congregation.

PASTORAL PRAYER

It must be long and presents the assembly to God. It must include:

1. Worship and praise
2. Confessions
3. Queries, supplications, or petitions
4. Intercessions
5. Thanksgiving or acknowledgments
6. Dedications

BENEDICTION

It can be done standing up for the simple reason that it is directed to the people and not to God. It invokes God, it is true, but on the people.

OFFERTORY PRAYER

It must be short, asking the Lord to accept the offerings and impart on children the gift of fidelity and the spirit of sacrifice.

SCRIPTURE READING

The reading must be excellent. He or she must read slowly and pay attention to the punctuation.

PRAYER MEETING

Prayer meetings take place mostly during the week. In the large assemblies, there are various groups of prayers: deacons, women, youth, officers of other departments, etc. All these prayer meetings have a special purpose: research the power of the Holy Spirit, consecration, issuing, members' concerns, etc.

These meetings are important: more prayer, more power. The meditations or studies in the prayer meetings must be short, prepared and illustrated.

The objective of a prayer meeting is the prayer. Otherwise the plans and goals are mixed. It is well to sing first to help attain an attitude of prayer. It is not a service of singing. Everyone must know why they will pray.

A person can come to a prayer meeting with a specific need or to have more relationship with God.

ANNOUNCEMENTS

These will be short and brief, made with sufficient clarity to avoid repetition. The announcements must be given to the responsible person to handle in the allotted time, in proper order, and as simply as possible.

BIBLE STUDIES

These are not worship services. Singing must be kept to a minimum. While these are not prayer services, prayer must be made to invoke the divine assistance.

May our service be agreeable to God!

6

EVANGELISM DEPARTMENT

P astor Gérald Guiteau, one of the most prominent preachers of Haiti, has reported in his book, the declarations of Russel P. Spittler that the baptism of the Holy Spirit created missionaries, not theologians.[15]

John the Baptist announced that the mission of Christ would be to baptize with the Holy Spirit and with fire. And Jesus said to his disciples that they would be baptized with the Holy Spirit, and they would be his witnesses to the ends of the earth. Furthermore, the apostle Paul, in 2 Corinthians 5.20, said that we are doing the duties of ambassadors for Christ. We are all invited into the power of the Holy Spirit, and we must engage in the mission of the conquest of souls.

A. Introduction to Evangelism
1. **The visitors/evangelists**
   Must have the following characteristics:
   a. Preparation of the heart, spirit and life. They must have a purified heart before God.
   b. Passion for the unsaved (that is the basis of the prayer for the unsaved). They must memorize verses, live holy lives.
   c. Persistence, to be able to make the unsaved understand that if they continue to reject Christ, it could be too late. It is better to enter the kingdom of God today.
   d. Power. The work of evangelism is done by the power of the Holy Spirit, which regenerates, convinces and seals.
   e. Invocation (argument). Leave the people to feel the attractive quality of Christ through you.

---

[15] Gérald Guiteau, *The Pentecostalism in Haiti,* page 113

2. The Contact

- Way to approach
  1. Be simple in your words.
  2. Be friendly, compassionate.
  3. Be optimistic.
- Place of meeting
  1. At school (attention to the hours of class).
  2. At work (pay attention to work hours/schedule).
  3. In the street.
  4. In a restaurant.
  5. At the doors of houses. Let them know why you are there.
  6. At the church.
- The conversation

  1. General Suggestions
     a) Have knowledge of general semantics, the words are important.
     b) In case of offense, be quick to apologize.
     c) Be a good listener.
     d) When two are visiting together, decide who goes first before reaching the person or the house.
     e) Do not go off topic in trying to respond to all the questions, because some issues can be used to divert the conversation.
     f) Support as a witness staff for Christ.
     g) Arrange your conversation as well:
- Christ
- Christian home
- Member of the church
     h) If you cannot decide on a place to meet, you can make an appointment. If you must change, make it in advance.
     i) Talk to one person at a time.
     j) If the person decides, call company to help spread the news.
     k) Do not use too many verses, to avoid confusion

  2. Specific Suggestions
     o Become a Christian
        i) A change of mind (repentance)

           ii)   A change of direction (conversion)

           iii) A change in conversation (confession)

           iv) A change of confidence (belief in Christ)

   o   Avoid

           i)   An uncontrolled tone of voice

           ii)   Any joking attitude toward problems discussed

           iii) Criticism of churches and pastors

           iv) The suggestion that the reformation can be done without Christ

           v)   Forcing or rushing the discussion

           vi) Doctrinal disputes

           vii) Belief in yourself instead of the power of the Holy Ghost

The necessary passages referring to evangelism to observe the imperative of the Master that theologians call the Great Commission. The people involved must have knowledge of the passages on evangelism in the New Testament.

a.   The function and the work of the evangelist in the New Testament: Eph. 4.11; 2 Tim. 4.5; Mt. 28.19, 20

b.   The pastor-evangelist in the New Testament: 2 Tim. 4.5

c.   Lay evangelists in the New Testament: Acts 8.1; Phil. 4.2,3

d.   The place of women in evangelism in the New Testament: Jn 4; 2 Tim 1.5

e.   The local church in evangelism in the New Testament: Phil. 1.1; Apoc. 1, 2, 3

f.   Prayer and intercession in evangelism in the New Testament: Lk. 5.15, 16; Acts 9.11

g.   The work of the Holy Spirit in evangelism in the New Testament: Jn 3.5; 16.8-11

h.   The place of the message in evangelism in the New Testament: Acts 2.14-41

i.   Personal testimony in evangelism in the New Testament: Acts 1.8; 8.1, 4

j.   The doctrines of the cross and the resurrection in evangelism in the New Testament: Jn 3.16; Rom. 3.25; Acts 17.32

k.   The place of the Word of God in evangelism in the New Testament: 1 Pet. 1.24, 25; 2 Tim. 3.16, 17

l.   Miracles and evangelism in the New Testament: Jn 2.11, 23; Acts 8.6

m. Satanic forces and evangelism in the New Testament: 2 Cor. 4.4, 5; Acts 26.18
n. The plan of God for world evangelism taught in New Testament: Mt. 28.19; Eph. 3.7-9
o. Differences between the conditions of evangelism in the time of the New Testament and ours.

B. Personal Evangelism (cure of soul)

The person responsible for evangelism must have knowledge of the following topics:

1. A lost soul
2. Unbeliever, its nature and its causes
3. A saved soul
4. How can man be saved?
5. Baptism and evangelism
6. Assurance of salvation
7. Personal evangelism in the New Testament
8. The Christian's responsibility for the lost
9. The satanic opposition to the efforts of winning souls
10. The importance and the benefits of personal evangelism
11. The contributions of psychology, psychiatry and the modern counselor
12. The conditions of success for winning souls
13. The principles of personal evangelism
14. Employment of the Bible in personal evangelism; how and when someone memorized the scripture
15. How to approach contacts
16. Class for the members working in the field
17. The twenty-one categories of souls
    a. Seekers wishing to be saved: Isa. 53.6; Jn 1.12.17; 3.15, 16.36; 1 Jn 5:18
    b. Too bad, too great sinner: 1 Tim. 1.15; Lk. 19.10; Rom. 5.8; 10.13; Jn 3.16; Mt. 9:12-13
    c. Not good enough: Isa. 53:12; Mt. 9:13; Lk. 15:7; 19:10; Rom. 5:8
    d. Indifferent, unconcerned: Rom. 3:23; Isa. 55:6; Acts 17:27
    e. Not interested, unloved: Isa. 55:6; Phil. 2:21; Ps 145:20
    f. Fear, hesitation: 2 Tim. 2:12; Phil. 2.14
    g. Those who base their hope of salvation on their Christian morality and their good conduct: Gal. 3.10; Jas 2.10
    h. Fear of being dropped, relapsed: 1 Pet. 1.5; Jn 10:28-29; Jude 24

      i.   Not today: Isa. 55.6-8; Prov. 29.1; Mt. 24:44

      j.   Love of the world, too much renunciation to do: Mk 8.36; Acts 9.5; Heb. 3.7-8

      k.   Fear of being ridiculed and persecuted: 2 Tim. 2.12; Rom. 8.17; 2 Cor.4.9; Mk 8.38

      l.   The Christian life is too difficult: Mt. 10.30; Prov. 3.17; 1 Jn 3.5

      m.   Too many hypocrites in the Church: Lk. 15:2; 2 Tim. 2.19

      n.   Cause of my work: Lk. 16.9

      o.   I have committed the unforgivable sin, or it is too late: 2 Cor. 6.2; Lk. 23.39-43

      p.   I want neither baptism, nor to be a member of an assembly: Heb. 10.25; Mt. 28.19

      q.   Doubter, skeptical: 1 Cor. 1.18; 2.14; Jn 7.17

      r.   I am a member of the Church: Jn 3.36

      s.   Former member of the Church: Jn 1.12

      t.   Sick and afflicted: Job 5.18; Ps 103.3; Ps 34.19

      u.   Agnostic, atheist: Ps 13.1; Mt. 24.35; Lk. 24.27, 1 Cor. 2.8; Heb. 1.8; Jn 20.28; 1 Jn 2.22-23; Apoc. 1.18

18. How to grow in grace after having accepted

C. Evangelism and the Local Church

"Go therefore and make disciples of all nations..." (Mt. 28.19). The church, in adequate conditions, must have a well-developed program of evangelism.

1. The plan of God for the local church.
2. The evangelical church, its role.
3. The leader in example of evangelism.
4. Organization of the church for evangelism.
5. Prayer and the Holy Spirit in evangelism, or prayer and alarm clocks.
6. Organization of evangelism visits, touring missionaries.
7. Cooperation with other organizations in evangelism.
8. Evangelism in the Sunday school.
9. Evangelism of young people.
10. Evangelism of children.
11. Classes for teaching members.
12. Extension of evangelism of the church to schools, outdoors, etc.
13. Evangelism by literature or tract.
14. Table and advertising evangelism.
15. Evangelism in rural areas.
16. Evangelism from house to house.
17. Meetings of evangelical union.

18. Conservation and use of evangelical results.

D. Evangelism from the pulpit

The responsible person must consider the following points:

a. Sunday evening service
b. Gaining opportunities
c. Factors of influence
d. Success meaning
e. Methods for a better service on Sunday evening
   1. Gospel music
   2. Evangelical meetings in the church
   3. Gospel message
   4. Evangelical invitations
   5. After service invitations
   6. Evangelism by radio
   7. Evangelist vocations; appeal, qualifications, conduct, methods, opportunities.
   8. Evangelism of home
   9. Evangelism outdoors
   10. Evangelism in the industries, the markets, the factories, etc.

E. Evangelism department committee

In normal conditions, the department must have:

1. An executive committee
   a. A manager
   b. A secretary
   c. A treasurer
   d. A delegate
2. A sub-committee of planning for: the revivals, crusades, companions of evangelists
3. A sub-committee of devotions

This committee is responsible to pray for the success of the department

4. A sub-logistics committee

In case of missionary programs, this committee must deal with the means of housing

5.   A sub-committee for visitation

Its role is to provide advice and take the results in the visits to homes.

Go therefore, make disciples of all nations….

7

WOMEN'S DEPARTMENT

W omen in the church are often ignored under the pretext that the Apostle Paul had reduced them to silence. There are often more women than men in the church. In the majority, they spend more time in the work of God than men. The ministry of women in the church is encouraged by certain fellows and discouraged by the other fellows. Discussing the topic considering the Word, this is not the first time that the Church has had differences. The Council of Jerusalem was held because of differences between the apostles chosen by Jesus Christ. Even today, theologians are not unanimous on the meaning of the message of Paul. The writings of Paul have posed problems before now, even for people filled with the Holy Spirit. The Apostle Peter, for example, a man full of the Holy Spirit, had difficulty understanding some of the writings of Paul. "as also in all his epistles, speaking in them of these things, in which are some things hard to understand..." (2 Pet. 3.16). To clarify this point, we are going to explore the historic part of the ministry of women and the conflicting points.

A. Women's ministry historically

Considering first the leaders in the Old Testament.

The people of Israel were formed by three groups of leaders: the priests, the wise men, and the prophets (Jer. 18.18).

1. The priests; three essential tasks:
   a. Serve the Lord in the temple: Ex. 28.30; Num. 18.1, 21
   b. Consult the Lord for the people by means of the Urim and Thummim: Ezra 2.63; Num. 27.21; Isa. 28.6
   c. Teach the people: 2 Chr. 15.3

2. The wise: they shall endeavor, through observation, experience, reflection, to reach to know the man and God. Wisdom, the expression of good sense, is a gift of God. It involves the fear of the Lord and obedience to his commandments. (Ps 111.10; Pr. 9.10; Eccl.12.13). The wise are people who can identify in their experiences some recurring principles. They can predict the future in each situation. There is always a prophetic aspect to the wisdom. For example, Daniel was a wise man in Babylon. The wise had three essential missions:
   a. Seek and search with care all that is done: Eccl.1.13; Dan. 9.2
   b. Survey everything that is done: Eccl. 1.13; Dan. 9.2
   c. Teach the people: Eccl.1.12; 12.11; Dan. 11.33 The Hebrew word "Koheleth" which translated "the Ecclesiastes" means teacher.

3. The prophets, according to the **New Bible Dictionary Emmaus**:" the one that God empower to his authority to communicate its willingness to men and instructing them." The prophets had three essential missions:
   a. Give the messages of God to the people: Deut. 18:18
   b. Serve as watchmen to the people: Jer. 6:16-17
   c. Teach the people: Jer.18:18, Eph. 2:20

The Hebrew word "nabhi' is the same word that is translated prophet: 1 Sam. 10:5; 19:20; 1 Kings 20:25. This word has a feminine form, "Nabhi'â," which means prophetess, New American Standard Bible, Hebrew and Greek of the Bible page 75.5031. This same root we find for the word disciple. And even the definition of the word prophet told us that he was an instructor.

Therefore, if the Apostle Paul has not removed the right of being a prophet from the woman, he cannot remove the right to teach from the women either. We need a lot of care, my friends, in studying the writings of Paul, because Jesus said in the Choosing: "... is my chosen instrument ..." (Acts 9:15). In the past, this man caused a lot of problems by the things he has said. He divided the assembly of the Sanhedrin by declaring that he was a Pharisee (Acts 23:6-7). He confused King Agrippa by asking him to become a Christian like him, except for the chains he was wearing (Acts 26:29). We are determined to go in the direction of the truth.

There were many women prophets in the Old as well as in the New Testament, such as: Mary, Huldah, Deborah, and the four virgin daughters of Philip (Acts 21:19). Women had been accepted in history as prophets.

Then, the prophets' ministry included teaching, therefore, women prophets were teachers. The Apostle Paul could not prevent them from teaching.

Therefore, my beloved in the Lord, do not withhold the hand of God going forward. We see clearly that women can exercise their talents in the church.

B. The Conflicting Points
The texts relating: 1 Cor. 11.2-16; 14.33-38; 1 Tim 2.9-15; Phil. 4.2-3; 1 Cor. 14.34-35

It is clear according to 1 Cor. 11.5 that women prayed and prophesied in the assemblies. It is also clear, according to chapters 12-14 that the women have received the spiritual gifts and are encouraged to exercise them in the body of Christ. In the Corinthian culture, women were not allowed to confront the men in public. Apparently, some women who were becoming Christians thought that their Christian freedom gave them the right to question the men in public service. This had created a division in the church of Corinth. In addition, the women of the time were not receiving a formal religious education as much as men. The women of the time would seem to address in the services issues that needed to be answered at home. Paul asked the women not to abuse their Christian freedom. Paul says in 1 Cor. 10:23, "I have the right to do anything, "you say -- but not everything is beneficial. "I have the right to do anything" -- but not everything is constructive. Therefore, the words of Paul to the Corinthians were a call to unity and not a ban on the women in ministry.

Regarding the church of Ephesus, in 1 Tim. 2.9-15.

"In the first-century Jewish culture, women were not allowed to study. When Paul said that women should 'learn quietly and submissively,' he was offering them an amazing opportunity to learn God's word. That they were to listen and learn quietly and submissively referred to an attitude of quietness and composure (not total silence). In addition, Paul himself acknowledges that women publicly prayed and prophesied (1 Cor.11:5). Apparently, however, the women in the Ephesian Church were abusing their newly acquired Christian freedom. Because these women were new converts, they did not yet have necessary experience, knowledge, or Christian maturity to teach those who already had extensive scriptural education"[16].

In this same letter, Paul explained to Timothy that he should not appoint people without honorable virtues, in 1 Tim 3.1-13. Women of Ephesus were not ready to discern the truth from the false teachings that

---

[16] *New Living Translation Bible, page 2691.*

were circulating at the time. They were such that they wore inappropriate clothing, and they were the targets of false teaching. Priscilla, a fellow laborer with Paul, taught the great preacher Apollos, according to Acts 18.24-26. Paul mentioned a few women who occupied the same functions in the Church such as: Phoebe (Rom. 16.1); Tryphena and Tryphosa, Persis (Rom. 16.12); Euodia and Syntyche (Phil. 4.2).

Now how do we see the women's department?

1. Role of the department

    a.   Appeal and enrollment
    b.   Missionary education
    c.   Bible study and devotion services
    d.   Development work
    e.   Social services and inspiration
    f.   Evangelism
    g.   Services of dinner.
    h.   Christian friendships
    i.   Home meeting
    j.   Day care
    k.   Care of clothing in the choir, communion supplies, baptismal equipment.
    l.   The intake of flowers
    m.   Counselors
    n.   Assistance to the christening ceremony
    o.   Organization of conferences
    p.   Organization of evangelism campaigns
    q.   Cure of soul
    r.   Organization of artistic and cultural activities
    s.   Organization of the programs for the poor

6. Ways to collect funds

Donations to the group must be made in good conditions.

7. The status of the group

    a.   Choose a Christian name for the group.
    b.   Describe in detail the objectives of the group.
    c.   Define the rules for the members of the group.
    d.   Define the tasks of each leader.
    e.   Plan the time of meeting.
    f.   Specify the method of elections.

g. Accommodate the laws of the church.
h. Define the women's committee.
i. The duration of the committee mandate.

8. The women's committee

The committee will expand or contract depending on the size of the church. In a big assembly, one can have several women's groups, several committees. In a small assembly, we can have a single women's group, a single committee. In the case of a large assembly, apart from the various committees, we must have a central committee above all these committees.

a. Suggestion for the committee
 1. President
 2. Vice-president
 3. Secretary
 4. Treasurer
 5. Delegates
b. Duration of the mandate of the committee is defined as for the other committees of the church in Chapters 3 and 4.
c. Selection of members of the committee is following the formula adopted: election or appointment.
d. Qualifications of the members of the committee as treated for the Sunday school department.
e. The same requirements as to the other committees of the church treated in Chapters 3 and 4.
f. Role of the committee: to work for the respect of the organization and the observation of its laws.

9. Sub-committees

a. Prayer committee
It is there to pray for the services of the church, for the leaders, the newly baptized, newly converted, and the needs of the people.
b. Communion committee
It is there to take care of the supplies and of the equipment of communion.
c. Maintenance committee
It is responsible for the maintenance of the church.
d. Planning committee

It must plan the activities concerning the women's department.
e. Devotional committee

This committee is responsible for promulgating the programs of conferences, Bible studies, seminars etc.

10. The pastor and the women's department

a. The pastor must participate in at least one meeting of the women's department.
    He must do so in agreement with the president of the women's department.
    He can offer his service to the women's department.

b. The pastor and the committee may organize a dinner with the members of the committee.

"The women who announce the news are a great host" Ps 68.11

8

YOUTH DEPARMENT

According to history, the organization of the youth in the church gives an opportunity for youth to develop under the gaze of Christian leaders.

A. The organization
a. The organization is for better cooperation between young people.
b. A platform where young people can learn to think.
c. A place where the young develop their rhetoric in the Word of God.
d. An altar where the young bring their consecration.
e. A passage to the future.
f. A place to find Christian friends.
g. A place of prayer or where the young listen to the voice of God.
h. A place for the young Christian to break in his convictions.

B. Objectives
a. Develop young leaders.
b. Give opportunities to young people to plan Christian programs.
c. Grant special attention to young people and give them opportunity to receive them.
d. Organize programs: Lessons, drives, bible studies missions, evangelism, devotions, social events.
e. Provide an opportunity for young people to appear in the other departments of the church.
f. Work to meet the needs of young people. (spiritual and social)
g. Help the young people to be loyal to Jesus Christ

h. Assist young people in understanding the meaning of prayer and worship.
i. Help young people to go further through the study of the Word of God.
j. Serve the church.
k. Meet other young people in other churches for active programs.

C. Launching of the Organization

a. The steps

1. Obtain the interest and enthusiasm of a few leaders of young people.
2. Seek prospective members and leaders of the church who are available.
3. Organize a meeting. Use the means available to have several young people who can be considered as prospective members.
4. At the meeting, present the opportunities and the plans of the organization.
5. Use an appropriate method (voting, census) to find out if the organization is acceptable.
6. Decide the time of meetings and the ages who can be involved.
7. Choose an organization committee for the formulation of the status of the organization.
8. Aim for simplicity, unity, and flexibility.

b. The Committee

1. The committee may have a president, vice-president, secretary, treasurer, and two delegates (if necessary).
2. The tasks of the committee.

The committee must meet before the major meetings in an appropriate period.

a. President

1. Lead the fulfilment of the program of the organization.
2. Be ready and able to help any officer or committee when the need arises.
3. Keep contact with other groups of young people.
4. Chair the meetings of the organization.

5. Avoid confusion in the work of other leaders and other committees.
6. Support a good reputation for the company.

b. Vice-President

1. Be a teammate and not a simple replacement for the president.
2. Seek ways of developing the organization.
3. Be prepared to replace the president during his absence.
4. In agreement with the president, supervise certain programs.

c. Secretary

1. Keep the list of the members and take notes of meetings.
2. Inform the president of the work.
3. Note the announcements of meetings and special meetings.
4. Notify the members of the committee of their tasks.

d. Treasurer

1. Receive the funds of the organization.
2. Be responsible for the security of the funds of the organization.
3. Be the official to spend the funds.
4. Be ready if an audit of the funds is recommended.

e. Delegates

1. Ensure communication between the committee of youth and other entities of the church and all the other institutions and personalities.
2. Ensure the purchase of equipment required for the organization

D. Sub-committees

For the proper functioning of the organization, sub-committees must be selected. We need to consider:

a. People of experience.
b. Members without experience, to give them an opportunity to learn.
c. Avoid attitudes that could cause the ruin of the organization

      d. Choose members with a spirit of friendship to create a good company of work.

1. The Missionary Committee
   Encourage and assist the missionary spirit and help to educate the organization in respect to missions.
2. The Social Affairs Committee
   Show the value of recreation in the development of Christian personality. Work for social development.
3. The Scheduling Committee
   Schedule meetings to provide the necessary materials for the meetings.
   Encourage the participation of any individual.

E. Meeting and Programs

  a. The essential aspects of the meetings.
1. The program must include the vital problems.
2. The program must have a goal.
3. The program can be done on a theme.
4. The program must be interesting.
5. The program must be planned and well prepared before the meeting.
6. The program should encourage the participation of members.
7. Leaders must measure up to the ideal Christian in their sincerity and be empowered to create a spirit of reverence.
8. The meetings should not be monotonous.

  b. Consideration in the choice of themes.
1. The themes should be interesting to young people.
2. The themes must be in logical order.

  c. Methods of presentation of themes.
1. Debates.
2. Panel discussion.
3. Dramatization.
4. Pantomime.
5. Round table.
6. Art.
7. Films.
8. Varieties.

  d. Types of Programs.
1. Historical studies.

2. Program of worship.
3. Missionary program.
4. Box of the questions.
5. Foreign guest.
6. Songs and stories of songs.
7. Study of parliamentary acts.
8. Bible studies.
9. History of the Church.
10. Demonstration.
11. The music service.
12. Installation service.
13. Service of consecration.

e. Meeting supplies.
    1. Topic or material of lesson.
    2. Bible.
    3. Concordance, dictionary, commentary.
    4. Book of songs.
    5. Projector.
    6. The aids of worship.
    7. Assistance with announcements.
    8. Piano.
    9. Recording devices.

f. The steps in planning the program.
    1. Prayer.
    2. Study the theme.
    3. Decide the objective of the meeting.
    4. Determine the method of presentation.
    5. Arrange the program in order and give a copy to participants if it is necessary
        a. Distribute responsibilities.
        b. Meeting presider.
        c. Pianist.
        d. Songs leader.
        e. Scripture reader.
        f. Prayer leader.
        g. Chair of special selections.
        h. Orator of the theme.
        i. Chair of the special features; poems, illustration, etc.
        j. Offering Collector.

      k.   Updates announcer

g.   Standards of the organization
    1.   The organization will have:
       a.   A goal.
       b.   A program.
    2.   Method of the Organization
       a.   Will adopt a constitution.
       b.   Shall elect officers for special tasks.
       c.   Will highlight the programs in advance.
       d.   Will hold regular meetings at specific times.
       e.   Will report progress to the body of the Church.
    3.   Meetings are planned.
    4.   The meetings are scheduled with other members of the group.
    5.   The meetings are based on the needs of the group.
    6.   The meetings are varied as to the theme and presentation.
    7.   The meetings are coordinated with the worship and the theme.
    8.   The meetings are correlated to the theme from the beginning to the end.
    9.   The meetings are held in a suitable place with the members of the organization.
    10. The development staff must show:
       -   A magnification of personality.
       -   A sense of responsibility to the needs of others
       -   A development of personal talents.

Catch all the foxes......for the grapevines are blossoming!

9

MEN'S DEPARTMENT

This department must be a place of comfort, a place to form allies (prayer, worship, friends) in a world sometimes so broken, unfriendly. A place of welcome that makes a difference. A place where the majority wants to be. A place where people have a chance to express themselves without fear of anybody. A place to share the emotions too often marginalized -- tenderness, complete joy, love, secret needs.

This is a group that attends to the needs of the people and sympathizes with them by helping them to overcome their enemies. A group to combat solitude, sadness, and to teach the beautiful human virtues. A group that gives the impression that they deserve their affection. A group that wishes to bring out what the world seems to forget: duty, loyalty, respect. A group that will provide its members with the means to cope with challenges, especially in times of disasters of all kinds. The group must be reliable.

A. The Reason for the Department
According to statistics published in 2013 by **Church Of Good Life Builders**:

Out of 10 men in a church:
9 will have children who leave the church
8 will not find their work satisfactory
5 have a major problem with pornography
4 will be divorced, affecting 1,000,000 children per year.

85 percent of the lay department people in the local churches are women
80 percent of the members of the group of prayers are women
60 percent of young leaders are women

- When a child is the first person to come to Christ, the rest of the family will follow 31 percent of the time.
- When a mother is the first person in the family to come to Christ, the rest of the family will follow 17 percent of the time.
- When a man is the first person to come to faith in Christ, the rest of the family will follow 93 percent of the time.

The benefits of a men's department:

a. Touch the men on the periphery of the church
b. Make disciples and develop leaders.
c. Mobilize men of the church to work for the advance of the kingdom of God.
d. Help men to form small cells/ work groups or Bible study groups.
e. Develop mentors
f. Strengthen the family
g. Begin the magnification of the men in the faith[17]

B. Methods of recruitment

1. Choose people with a spirit of leadership to continue the incomplete work.
2. Plan a recruitment campaign with each class of people to reach all the people.
3. Work on appropriate methods to reach more young people.
4. Give defined responsibilities to men.
5. The key to success is the management of people.

C. Program

1. The program must touch all the people of the church.
2. The program must be rich and attractive.

D. The Committee of the Department

The committee will expand or contract depending on the size of the church. In a big assembly, one can have several groups of men, several committees. In a small assembly, we can have a single group of men, a single committee. In the case of a large assembly, to share the various committees, we can have a central committee above all these committees.

---

[17] Source: *coglife builders.com*

1. Suggestion of committees.
   a. President
   b. Vice-president
   c. Secretary
   d. Treasurer
   e. Prefects of disciplines
   f. Advisors
   g. Delegates
2. The duration of the mandate of the committee is defined as for the other committees of the church.
3. The choice of the members of the committee is made following the adopted formula: election or appointment
4. The qualifications of the members of the committee are the same requirements as for the other committees of the church.
5. The role of the committee.
   a. Collaborate with the pastor responsible
   b. Plan with the pastor responsible for the development of the department.
   c. Work for the respect of the organization and the observation of these laws.
   d. Encourage attendance in the church.
   e. Create a climate of brotherhood between the brothers and bring back the defective.
   f. Establish a harmonious relationship between the pastor and the men.
   g. Think about the needs of other entities of the church (women, youth, etc.).
   h. Organize campaigns of evangelism.
   i. Extend the group.
   j. Cooperate in community activities.
   k. Organize conferences.
   l. Encourage love and acceptance.
   m. Encourage the work of the church
   n. Encourage members to be good citizens of the community (Christian and non-Christian), Peter 2:13-14.

E. The Sub-Committees

The sub-committees are chosen as for the other sub-committees of the church.

F. Ways to Collect Funds

The donations to the group must be made in good condition as for the other departments of the Church.

A man after God's heart will do his will.

10

CHILDREN'S DEPARTMENT

I t is necessary that the Church think of everyone in the world: rich or poor, young or elderly, educated or illiterate, men or women, religious or irreligious, moral or immoral, adults or children. Christ took the time to talk to the Pharisees, to the scribes, to Nicodemus, a confused leader, to Nathanael in whom he found no guile, to modest Andrew, to Matthew the tax collector, to the Samaritan woman, to Zacchaeus the tax collector, to the thief on the cross, and to children who had been brought to him.

The Church must not neglect any sector of its components. The Word said we are to raise children in the way that they must follow, and when they are grown, they will not depart from it.

The importance of this department is as clear as crystal in the teaching of Christ. The Synoptic Gospels clearly show the manifestation of the tenderness of Christ toward the children as part of the community of the kingdom. We must not neglect the kingdom of God, which is for those who resemble children. We are all in contact with children at one time or another, and we know that children are a blessing of God.

A. Objective

The department must have a clear ideal of working to guide the children toward Christ and to make them cooperate with him. The families of Israel received the order to teach the Word of God every day in their homes. The Bible says:" And these words that I command you today shall be in your heart. You shall teach them diligently to your children, and shall talk of them when you sit in your house, and when you walk by the way, and when you lie down, and when you rise" (Deut. 6.6-7). The Bible says that we will have trials and tribulations in life, however, it has not told us to face the combat alone.

B. Leader

Social status was of great importance in the ancient culture. This has not changed much; he that has the gift of ministration, let him minister (Rom.12.7).

C. Qualifications of Leaders

1. Accountable.
    Submission to the authorities of the church is an indispensable condition for the leaders of children.
2. Jovial.
    Leaders must be happy to be with the children. The leaders must have an unconditional love for the children.
3. Lenient.
    It is necessary that the leaders are ready to forgive.
4. Humble.
    Humility precedes glory. The leader must create conditions of work where the children feel comfortable.
5. Compassionate/Patient.
    Leaders must show a warm love for children, a willingness to sacrifice, to go until the end. They must not neglect extra meetings if they are necessary to succeed in a good work.
6. Prompt to Listen.
    The leaders must always be ready to listen to the children. They must show a strong desire in this.

D. Role of leaders

1. Help children to participate in the kingdom of God.
    In John 6:9, we find a child who has offered his food to Jesus for the multiplication of the loaves.
2. Create interesting programs.
    If the programs are boring, children will not participate. The promise is for you, for your children, and for all those who are far away in as many as the LORD our God will call.
3. Seek the potential of each child by observation.
4. Progress from time to time.
    Work to become better from day to day. Create new ideas. Participate in seminars ... maintain a good relationship with parents. Develop children to become committed to Christ.

E. Reach unbelievers

They must create conditions where the children feel comfortable to invite their friends.

F. Complementary mission

The department of children must be in line with the mission of the Church.

G. Spiritual maturity

1. Thanks

   The department of children must work in development of the grace given to children to create opportunities for evangelism. These opportunities are present especially in the purposes of weeks where the children invite their friends to the church. Other special events offer other opportunities.

2. Magnification.

   Work for a revolution caused by the faith of the children. They must show children how they must: walk in Christ, rooted and grounded in Christ, and consolidate by the faith after the instructions they have received and abound in shares of graces.

3. Grouping.

   Small groups are very safe for children. Small groups serve as a perfect arrangement for adults to help the children to apply the lessons of the day in their lives and connect to the model of the Christian community. The leader has a privilege and a responsibility because she is with them each week, and is their model.

4. Donations.

   Offer opportunities for children to explore their gifts and to observe the model of adults of the church.

5. Good stewardship.

   Teach children that all they have belongs to God. They must teach them to work against greed and self-indulgence.

H. Programs for Children

1. Songs.

   Find appropriate music and songs that will interest the children.

2. Education.

   If education is necessary to teach things that the children will be able to understand, the teaching must be relevant and oriented.

3. Special Programs.

   Any program must be a program of rejoicing for children.

   a. The space.

       1.   Well ventilated.
       2.   Good décor.
       3.   Filled with things that appeal to children.
       4.   Safe.
    b. Methods of teaching.

Apply creativity to teach the Bible so children can understand it instead of bearing it. They must not be too sentimental nor too much fun.

I. Division of children.

Each child must be part of a group. In small assemblies, they are mixed. In the large assemblies, they are subdivided:

2-3 years
4-5 years
6-8 years
9-11 years

    1.   Types of programs vary for the different categories:
       a. 2-3 years: jump inching, walking, movement of hands. These movements must be without precision and individuality. Any simple movement is recommended.
       b. 4-5 years: race from one point to another, send and catch balls.
       c. 6-8 years: songs, games of varieties, games of large movement are encouraged.
       d. 9-11 years: team games with fixed rules are encouraged.

Let the children come to me

11

THE PASTOR AND THE MEMBERS

A. Visit from House to House

S ometimes the situations of life make us forget our call. He that has the gift of ministration, let him minister (Rom.12.7). Our calling is final, because God does not repent of his gifts nor of his call. The pastor must do his best to keep contact with the people by teaching them, by visiting, and by meetings. The pastor must try to become a part of the life of each member. The shepherd spends his time with the sheep. The visits and friendships are two methods used to bind the people and the pastor. Try to get to know their needs to better serve them with your advice. The visit is a way to keep the fire of the gospel up. Do not neglect to visit the members.

1. The various reasons for the visit
   a. Informal visit.
   b. Visit optimist.
   c. Systematic tour.
   d. Impartial visit.
   e. Friendly visit.
   f. Evangelistic visit.
   g. Persistent visit.

2. Implementation of the visitation program
   a. Announce the next visit with the address and all necessary information.

b. Send a message to tell them that you will be at their home for a precise time.

c. Sometimes, you must call.

d. Sometimes, it would be wise to invite a family to a meal.

e. Have a site visit committee.
   - The method of Jesus was two by two.
   - Pay attention to the choice of the people to send. Sometimes the envoys have forgotten the objective of the visit, especially if they are husband and wife.

f. Enjoy certain occasions, such as a birthday, to visit the home of a member.

g. At the news of a death in the membership, visit as soon as possible.

h. When the pastor visits a home and that person is not present, leave a card from the church with a memo.

i. Sometimes in an emergency, you are compelled to pray on the phone with the person.

j. There is no visitation late night, except in cases of emergency or by request.

3. Programming of visit

a. Schedule a list of visits to do.

b. Who is given priority?
   1. The sick
   2. Troubled persons
   3. To evangelistic perspectives
   4. Members in general

c. Tap and ring continuously.

d. If there is no way to enter, manage the conversation from outside without letting it frustrate you.

e. When entering, it would be good to remove shoes if they will dirty the house, and do not relax, you are not at home.

f. Talk informally to put the members at ease.
   1. Ask for the family and talk about the family.
   2. Discuss the general activities of the church
   3. Arrive at the point of the visit and speak of the Lord. The visit should last approximately twenty minutes.

g. Pray always before the visit, but not always during the visit. Read two or three verses and made a short prayer. If there are people present not from your church, ask if you can pray for the whole house. Use a lot of tact, do not require that members kneel. Pray always in the visits. In the hospital, pray for peace, strength, tranquility, and the rest of the evening. Let the Spirit guide you what is best of all.

h. In a new church
   1. Visit the officers and members of the church first.
   2. Then undertake the ministry of evangelism in general.

i. When you visit people at a time when they are occupied in any way, ask if you need to return, or wait if possible.

j. Keep records of the visits. At the annual meeting, it would be good to give the report of visitation.

4. The qualities for a pastoral visit.

a. The pastor who spends a lot of time visiting may not have the time to properly prepare his sermon as he wants. However, the imperfections of his sermon will be covered by the love that develops in the visits.

b. The result of the visit often enough is not immediate.

c. The pastor becomes closer to the people.

d. The visit is the means to reach the neighborhood.

e. This is a better imitation of Christ who was going from place to place and from village to village.

5. The opportunities of the visit.

a. Read the Bible in the home.

b. Pray in the house.

c. Invite people to worship at the church.

d. Develop the Sunday school.

e. It is better imitation of Christ who went from city to city, from village to village, from place to place.

6. Visitation aids.

a. Invitation card, inviting people to church.

b. Note those who are not at home when you visit.

c. Members list.

d. Welcoming newcomers.

7. Example of assistance to the visit.

Welcome to the church...

Address of the Church...

If you are not yet a member of any church, the church_____

is very happy to count you among us. If you wish, please, give your address and all other information.

Some churches ask visitors to return the visitor record to the ushers, others require putting in the offering plate.

Visitor Sheet
Name: ....
Address:...
Phone:...
I am new in the community: ....
Add my name to the church:...
I am sick: ....
I need to talk to pastor:..
I need to become a Christian: ....
I am visiting for the first time:.......................................
I am age: Less than 18 years; 18-29 years; 30-45 years;
45-60 years; 60+ years: ....

Recruitment for the services
Name:...
Address:...
Phone:...
Occupation:..
Section: young, adult, child:..
Are you baptized in water? Yes or No:............................
Profession: ....
Mark the field where you want to serve:.........................
Body of deacons: ....
Body of deaconesses:..
Administrative body: ....
Teaching body: ....
Missionary body:..
Body of ushers: ....
Other:..
Signature: ....
Date..

B. Visit to the hospital

Sick members always dream of receiving a visit from their pastor. Nothing can replace the visit.

The principles to be observed during the visit to the hospital

1. It is wise to talk to the doctor or to a person near the ill to know the nature and the state of the patient
2. Do not enter in conflict with the doctor.
3. You have a spiritual task.
4. Dress well for the visit.
5. Pray before the visit and during the visit. There will be cases where it would not be possible to pray during the visit. In praying do not raise your voice.
6. The pastor must bring his Bible to the visit.
7. The pastor must ask for permission to see the patient.
8. The pastor must obey the laws of the hospital.

The procedures to follow in a visit to the hospital

1. Do not sit on the patient bed.
2. Do not discuss your problems with the sick.
3. Do not speak with a loud voice. Do not joke, this may disturb the others.
4. Call the person in charge if the patient needs to raise or to return to the bed.
5. Do not visit at the time of the meal.
6. Do not leave any gifts of food without the authorization of the person in charge.
7. Do not be too long in the visit. Approximately fifteen minutes.
8. Do not ask questions that will embarrass the ill.
9. Always be happy, but not jovial.
10. Do not forget that the visit is spiritual.
11. Speak nicely to the people taking care of your member. If they are interested, some pastors invite them at the time of the reading and the prayer, some do not.
12. Obey the staff of the hospital.
13. Be positive and optimistic in your approach.
14. Be sincere in praying.
15. Visit the sick as many times as possible. The ill need you in this time.

C. Encouraging the attendance in the church

The shepherd must know in his spirit why people are interested in the church services. A church with a large workforce encourages the pastor, and encourages other people to join. The following items can help to have a good workforce participate in the services of the church.

1. The service must be well planned and executed.
2. The service must be edifying and reveal the glory of God in all its parts.
3. Welcome visitors so they feel at home. Some churches put individuals at the door to greet people. These people help visitors to find seats, and better understand the programs.
4. A well-organized visitation program encourages attendance in the Church.
5. Samples of the church program can be handed out during visitation.
6. A good evangelical emphasis.
7. A good Sunday lesson program.
8. Resolve the problems of the church whenever possible.
9. Arrange special gatherings on special occasions: birthdays, weddings, etc.
10. Be prepared to help interested parties to come to the service.
11. Hold a program of prayer for the congregation as well for prospective members.
12. Use a valid method to know the members and the addresses of the visitors.
13. Thank the people for their service, their presence in church.

D. Counseling ministry

The pastor can serve as an advisor to the young people for their relationship with God, their choice of a vocation and their choice of a partner for life. He can serve the family by advising on adjustment problems of marriage and the foundation of a Christian home. Also, he can help the sick, the aged and the afflicted. To advise these people, he should know the nature and the methods of giving advice.

Counseling is a process of cooperation between two people (counselor and counselee) who sit to consider a problem and apply their experience and wisdom in trying to find a solution.

Pastoral counsel is the activity of the pastor in which he tries by a variety of means to help his people to better understand that they can lead a happy life.

In pastoral counsel, the pastor will realize the benefits of employing the directive counseling and non-directive counseling. He will use one or the other in a situation where they are applicable.

1. Directive counseling

In this method, the counselor takes the initiative and poses questions to guide in finding important information. Understanding of this information will allow him to diagnose and to know the best decision for the person in question.

2. Non-directive counseling

This process assists individuals who suffer internal emotional conflict. They are embarrassed to live happily and effectively. This kind of counsel seeks to assist the individual to complete an overview of the problem, win an understanding of himself and of the problem, manage the emotional tension, and make wise decisions.

3. The major problems in the employment of direct counsel

It is true that this method is quick and less expensive, but it does not respond to two types of problems. The first type is the problem of a deep emotional nature. The behavior of a person who has need of attention most often originates in subconscious motives originating in a suppression of the person. Simple advice is inadequate without a clarification to bring release of the person. The second type of problem is about the responsibility to find a solution. In directing counsel pure; the counselor takes the responsibility to free the person of the situation, while the counselee takes a submissive role. This trend escalates as the situation of the patient worsens.

4. Group counseling

This process has the same objective as counsel by staff, but the counseling occurs within a group of people instead of between individuals. In a church situation, the group may be a board of education or administration, a class of young people or a group of adults.

5. A few steps in a process of counseling.

a.   Meeting place (s)

This is very important, and arrangements must provide the patient confidence and an adequate sense of security. Moses met with the people to the Tent of Meeting. "... Moses sat to judge the people: and the people stood by Moses from the morning unto the evening" (Ex. 18.13).

b. The prayer
    Ask God to guide you and help you to understand the problem." He who trusts in his own mind is a fool; but he who walks in the Wisdom will be delivered" (Prov. 28.26)

c. Collection of information
    Do not act in ignorance. Collect all the relevant information possible. Every prudent man deals wisely; but a fool speaks foolishness (Pr. 13:16).
    To answer a question before you have heard it out is both stupid and insulting (Prov. 18.13).
    Buy the truth, and do not sell wisdom, also buy understanding and instruction (Prov. 23.23).

d. Team principle
    If possible, share with a partner or a group. In this sense, you will have two combined experiences. Not only yours but also that of others.
    Take counsel when you form a plan, and have some policy when you make war (Prov. 20.18).

e. Principle of selection
    Ensure that you understand the reason and the objective of the decision. A man of understanding sets his face toward wisdom, but the eyes of a fool are on the ends of the earth (Prov. 17.24).

f. Principle of evaluation
    Evaluate the impact of the decision on the plan, internally and externally, individually and collectively.
    It is a danger to a man to say without thought, it is holy, and, after taking his oaths, to be questioning if it is necessary to keep them (Prov. 20.25).

g. Principle of preparation
    Prepare to approach the problem with serenity and certainty.
    A prudent man foresees the evil, and hides himself: but the simple pass on, and are punished (Prov. 22.3).

h. Principle of confrontation
    Be courageous to give the necessary counsel.
    Fear of man is a dangerous trap, but to trust in God means safety (Prov. 29.25).

i. The counsel or the decision
   When it is time to act, you must act with caution.
   Where no counsel is, the people fall: but in the multitude of counsellors there is safety (Prov. 11.14).

6 The specific objectives in the process of counseling.

   a. Identify the problem.
   b. Interpret the information and facts concerning the problem.
   c. Schedule possible solutions.
   d. Find a program adaptable to the plans.
   e. Change the plans to fit the circumstances.

7. The spirit of a motivating interview

According to "Association of pastoral counselors' methods of counselling," it is vital to distinguish between the spirit of a motivating and technical interview. On the other hand, the following points are established by Bingham and Moore in the process of an interview.

   a. Understand well the basic principles for the advisor.
   b. Have clearly in mind the main purpose of the interview.
   c. Get to know the interviewee and his past, until the past supports the central purpose of the interview.
   d. Expand and keep a good report for work.
   e. Help the person to see the problem involved and see clearly.
   f. Influence the client's attitude toward the solution of the problem.
   g. Center the interview on the client and his problem.
   h. Help the counselee to take steps toward the resolution of the problem.
   i. Help the teenager to develop increased empowerment to meet and solve similar problems on his own.
   j. Continue to see if the solution to the problem is completed.
   k. Make an adequate record of the interview.

E. Presentation of the Child at the Temple

Evangelical churches adopt the practice of presentation in the temple and not of the baptism of children. Why? Because baptism is a commitment in good conscience before God and before men. A newborn child is unable to make a commitment.

1. Before the ceremony
    a.   The pastor analyzes the marital status of the parents.
    b.   The parents present the birth certificate
    c.   The pastor examines the birth certificate.

2. The opening of the ceremony
This special service opens by an announcement made by the officiating pastor.
    a.   The invitation to the parents to be present with their child to the altar.
    b.   The officiant gives a brief meditation.
Such as:
Train up a child in the way he should go: and when he is old, he will not depart from it (Prov. 22.6).

3. Commitment of parents
Pastor: Do you present your child to God as a sacrifice of thanksgiving, and an offering of good odor?
Parents: Yes, we do, by the Grace of God
Pastor: Do you promise to raise your child in the teaching of the Word of God, in prayer, in adoration, so that at the appropriate time, he can accept Jesus Christ as his personal Savior?

4. Admonition to parents
The pastor says: Dear parents, since you promised before God and before this assembly to devote your child to God, to raise him in the way he must follow and lead an exemplary life, I will charge you, in the name of the Father and of the Son and of the Holy Ghost to faithfully fulfill and until the end your sacred commitment. May God, help you both!

5. Dedication of Children
The pastor takes the child in his arms and is assisted by other officers if there is more than one child.

6. Scripture reading
There is a whole series of appropriate reading such as:
-    1 Sam. 1.20, 24-28
-    Lk .2.21-40
-    Mk 10.13-16

7. Singing in common

There is a directory of appropriate songs.

8.Prayer of Consecration

The pastor invites the congregation to join him in a prayer of consecration.

Lord, author of all excellent graces, giver of every perfect gift; without your help, we can do nothing. In this solemn moment, we unite ourselves to these parents to present and devote this child that thou hast wanted to give to these parents. Let this child grow in the way that thou hast prepared for him. May he walk in the fear of thee, in obedience to thy voice. Let the parents perform their responsibilities toward him. That the life of the child be to thee a praise and glory. On behalf of Jesus Christ, our divine Savior we pray. Amen!

9. The pastor blesses the child and returns him to the parents

10. While the parents return to their seats, we can sing a hymn

11. Extra formalities

The registration of the date of the dedication in the Registry of the Church. A certificate of presentation will be prepared and presented to the parents of the children.

If your gift is that of serving others, serve them well!

12

THE PASTOR AND THE ORDINANCES

A. The Baptism and its Generality

1. **Training period of the candidate**

   The training is essential for laying a solid foundation: according to 1 Cor. 3.11, Jesus Christ is our foundation. We need to be fully implemented in this foundation to achieve maturity. The training has a biblical basis. In Mt. 28.19, Jesus also commanded: "Go and make disciples of all nations, baptizing them in the name of the Father, of the Son and of the Holy Spirit."

   The word "disciple" is a Latin word which means "student." If there is a student, there is teaching and the text continues to say after that to baptize them. So, we need a period of training. Some say that the Ethiopian eunuch was baptized at the same moment. There are unique cases in the Bible, like the case of the Apostle Paul.

   Remember, to be an apostle, he must be a witness to the activities of Jesus, of his death and resurrection. Paul was not there, but his apostolate was approved in a single case. Similarly, the Ethiopian eunuch was baptized in a single case. Baptism is a commitment, it may not be engaged in without knowing in what and why. Therefore, training is essential.

2. **The duration and the examination**

   If there is training, it must necessarily be a duration of training, any method to pass the necessary knowledge to students. If there is training, there must be some method of assessment or a way to approve or disapprove a candidate.

3. **Signs of immaturity**
   a. Weak understanding.
   b. Lack of responsibility.
   c. Lack of discernment.
   d. Instability

4. **The causes of immaturity**
   a. Compromise.
   b. Not really born again.
   c. Disobedience.
   d. Negligence of spiritual warfare.

5. **The doctrine of baptism**
   Baptism comes from the Greek "Baptizo," meaning dive or immerse.

6. **The different types of baptism**
   a. Baptism by spirit in a single body.
   This occurs at conversion, leading to the new birth. Jn 3.5. When a person goes to God, the Holy Spirit enters his life and revives the human spirit, which was dead spiritually, showing separation with God. (Rom. 8.9). The new believer, automatically accepted or immersed in the body of Christ, spiritually is placed in the proper place. Remember that the commitment of the believer toward the local church and the body of Christ is very important.
   Each member of the body has need of the other (2 Cor. 12.1-20) The body of Christ is a cover and a security for each member (Eph. 1.23-32)

   b. The baptism of the Holy Spirit
   In the baptism of the Holy Spirit, we receive the power of the Holy Spirit, who makes us capable of accomplishing the work of the ministry. We receive the baptism of the Holy Spirit by faith. This includes a request to God in the name of Jesus (Lk 11.13), by the imposition of hands (Acts 9.17).
   c. The baptism of fire
   This is when God brings things on our path to cleanse us. The moments of purging and purification come to us so that God can

change us and mold us to achieve the desired level for us (1 Pet. 1.12-19; 2 Tim. 2.3; Apoc. 2.10).

God can use the circumstances and the pressures of our life to complete this purification of our life. Unless we accept the purging of God, otherwise we will always be under the rod of infertility instead of accomplishing our full potential in Christ.

d. Water baptism

This is a ceremonial representation of the death, burial and resurrection of our Lord Jesus Christ. It shows that we share with Christ the fact of his death and his resurrection. It is an exterior manifestation of an interior grace.

The meaning of total immersion.

1. Total immersion means total annihilation of all the works of the devil or of the flesh. The Catholic practice of sprinkling means that the rejection is partial, but the Lord wants total surrender to him.
2. Total immersion implies that all members of the body are mortified (Rom. 6.4; Col.2.12).

7. The reasons for baptism

We must baptize.

1. Jesus required it (Mt. 28.19).
2. To accomplish any justice (Mt. 3.13-17).
3. It is a promise of a good conscience toward God (1 Pet. 3.21).
4. It is the functional doctrine of the early Church (Acts 2.41; 10.47-48).

8. The following confessions are made in the water baptism

1. To the heaven that we believe in the death, burial and resurrection of Jesus Christ (1Cor. 15.3-4).
2. To the Church of Christ, that we are members.
3. To the world: that we put an end to its actions.
4. To the Devil, that it is finished between him and us, and we have change camps to be the Bride of Christ. We are giving up our identification to the devil.

Note

The water baptism does not save the soul. It is faith in the death, burial and resurrection of Jesus Christ that can save the soul. Water baptism symbolizes this faith in Jesus Christ.

B. The Service of Baptism

The service of baptism is the result of the training, to the review and approval by the church of the candidates for baptism. Having been educated in the Word of God and having received the approval of the church, which makes of each candidate a favorable testimony, applicants present themselves in the church or in the place reserved at the baptism ceremony. Traditionally the candidates are dressed in white.

The baptistery should be large enough to hold at least two people. It should be placed so the audience can see the service and the participants. All necessary precautions concerning the place and the system of water, and a place to change clothing, must be prepared near the baptistery. It is important if two men can help in the changing room for men and two women for the women.

In the case of a single minister, he must be assisted by the deacons or elders of the church in the service of baptism.

1. Opening of the service

The officiant may open the ceremony by expression relating to the baptism such as:

Repent, and be baptized every one of you in the name of Jesus for the remission of sins (Acts 2.38).

Go therefore, make disciples of all the nations, baptizing them in the name of the Father and the Son and of the Holy Spirit (Mt. 28.19).

There is also an antitype which now saves us -- baptism (not the removal of the filth of the flesh, but the answer of a good conscience toward God), through the resurrection of Jesus Christ (1 Pet. 3.21).

2. Song of circumstance

We must sing hymns of consecration, songs that call to the Holy Spirit, songs that refer to the baptism.

3. Invocation prayer

Take account of the sacrifices of the candidates, the magnificence of God, of the grace of God.

A short prayer. Here is a model:

"Holy God, thy name is magnificent on the whole earth, exalted among men that thou hast created. In thee reside the grace, love, strength, courage, the blessing, the goodness. We exalt thee, O God. We ask you to approve and to bless this service, which is the answer to your order to empty the hell to fill the heaven. Grant our prayer that we address to you by Jesus Christ, your only Son. Amen.

4. Scripture reading

Read an appropriate text such as:
- Mt. 3.7-12
- Mt. 28.18-20
- Acts 28.26-39

5. Reflection on the baptism

The officiant takes a few minutes to explain to the assembly, particularly to applicants, the act that they wish to take.

6. The ceremony

a. Preparation of the pastor for the act of baptism
Now comes the time for the pastor to leave the chair to another pastor, to a deacon or a member to lead the assembly in songs chosen for the occasion. The assembly will continue to sing up to the end of the ceremony. The pastor or pastors officiating leave to change into clothes relating to the ceremony and step into the water.

b. Presentation of the applicants
The applicants will be held near the baptistery or near the water if the ceremony is held outdoors. Each candidate with a white towel or a white cloth is led to the officiant by a deacon.

c. Commitment of the applicants
The pastor will pose the following questions to each applicant to ensure their good faith before lowering them into the water of baptism:

Pastor: Do you believe that Jesus Christ, the only Son of God, died for your sins, in your place, he is risen from the dead and he is sitting now at the right hand of the Father now as your defender?

Applicant: Yes, I believe by the grace of God.

Pastor: Do you want to confess Jesus Christ before God and before men as your Savior and Lord?

Applicant: Yes, I am committed by the grace of God.

Pastor: Do you commit yourself to follow Jesus Christ in the good as well as the bad days and to conduct an exemplary life until the end of your earthly life?

Applicant: Yes, I will by the grace of God.

d. Pronunciation of the sacramental formula

The pastor will deliver one of the sacramental formulas:

Example: On this public confession of your faith in Jesus Christ our Savior and Lord, your commitment to follow up to the end, (some recommend mentioning the name of the sister or brother), I baptize you in the name of the Father, of the Son and of the Holy Spirit. Before the immersion, the pastor ensures that the applicant hold his breath and close his eyes to prevent water penetrating. After lifting the applicant from the water, he gives him to a person in charge who will lead him to the changing rooms.

e. Method of disposal

The pastor stands behind on the left shoulder of the applicant. The applicant then places both hands on his face above the level of the water. The pastor then places his left hand under the elbows to the arms of the applicant with his right foot behind the applicant and his right hand on the left shoulder of the applicant. The applicant is to bend his back until the minister immerses him in the water. Then, the pastor brings him back upright. Now the pastor can pass the applicant to a person in charge.

Prayer of intercession

Not to us, Lord, not to us, but unto thy name give glory, for thy loving-kindness, because of thy faithfulness! It is with a heart filled with joy, humility, trembling and recognition that we bow before thee in this time. We say thank you for these beloveds that thou hast redeemed from the curse of the devil and who now by your grace have shown their faith in the waters of baptism. We are asking you, God, to support them throughout their pilgrimage that they will respond favorably to their tasks, they walk in the way of their master and have an exemplary life. This is the prayer that we address in their favor in the name of Jesus Christ, your only Son, our divine Savior. Amen!

Benediction

The God of peace, who has brought back from the dead the great Shepherd of the sheep, by the blood of the eternal covenant, our Lord Jesus, make you capable of any good work for the fulfilment of its willingness; that it is in you this that are pleasing to him, through Jesus Christ, to whom be glory to the centuries of the centuries! Amen!

D. Formalities extra ceremonial

a. Registration in the official register of the church
After the baptism, a person responsible will save the names, dates of birth and the address of each newly baptized.

b. Baptism certificate
A certificate of baptism prepared and signed by the pastor of the church must be delivered to each newly baptized person in the name of the church.

E. Reception of New Members

a. A believer can become a member of a local church by:
a. Expressing publicly in a service of the church he is interested in.
b. The water baptism.
c. The adherence to the declaration of faith or profession of faith of the church or of the denomination.
d. The vote of the assembly or the executive board.
e. The affiliation on the recommendation of the last assembly of which the person was a member.

b. The reception service
If the baptized members and affiliates must be received at the same time, the local church must be informed in advance. The ceremony can be organized in a way to receive the two categories, or each category is received separately. In both cases, the order remains immutable. In general, the receipt of a new member normally takes place in the Sunday morning worship service, preferably on the day of communion, and the ceremony of communion takes place after.

c. The announcement
Brothers and sisters in Jesus Christ, we are presenting to you today as members in our church and in the name of Jesus Christ, brother/sister ------, or the beloved here. They have just manifested their

faith in the waters of baptism, or wish to join here and have been recommended by the central committee of the church or by the pastor (in the case of affiliation). We have the privilege to present them to you so that you can say openly whether you agree to let them join in our communion?

d. Presentation
In the case of the newly baptized:

Brothers and sisters in the Lord, you have demonstrated your faith in the waters of baptism as a sign of your commitment to Christ. In accepting this order, you say that Christ is your personal Savior, your Lord and your God. Please be aware that Christ died for us to be free to serve and that we can be members of the body that Christ has trained and which you have just asked today to join. Remember that those who are in Christ Jesus form a single body and are members of each other. Remember that Christ is the head of the Church and any other person, the Church owes him its submission according to the Scriptures, in matters of faith and religious belief.

In the case of an affiliation:

The pastor, after having completed the formalities (authenticity of the letter, role in the previous church, matrimonial condition, etc.), presents this or these members to the church.

Pastor: Brothers and sisters, do you want to become members of this church?

Affiliates: Yes, we want to.

Pastor: Do you promise to persevere in the teaching of the Word of God, in the communion of the saints and prayer?

Affiliates: Yes, we promise

Pastor: Do you promise to participate in all meetings of this church according to that God allows, you can pay your tithes and your offerings, to be a model?

Affiliates: Yes, we promise.

Pastor: In the name of Jesus Christ, the supreme head of the Church, we welcome you as full members of our assembly. We invite you to participate with us in the Lord's Supper.

e. Commitment of members to the church
By becoming members, you are part of the Body of Christ. Before God and before all, you take the commitment to walk according to the Scriptures in love, faith, and hope; to fight for the advancement of this church in wisdom, in holiness and consolation; to support its meetings, its orders and its discipline; to support this church in the work of the spreading of the Gospel.

f. Prayer of thanks
The pastor can do this prayer or his own.
We bless you, O God, for the salvation by faith in Jesus Christ that thou hast given us.
We bless you also for the sacrifice of Jesus Christ, your only Son, at Calvary and we thank you for your graces in our favor.
We thank you for the brother or the sister or these beloveds who join us today. Let his ministry or their ministry among us, be a blessing and that ours to him or them are also beneficial. Be with him/her/them, God, in any emergency, through the events, the perilous trails, the difficult circumstances. Fortify his faith/their faith and be his/her/their assistance in this new experience that he/she/they will do with us. We pray in the name of Jesus Christ, our divine Savior. Amen!

g. The hand of fellowship
The pastor as well as the officers of the church shake hands with each new member by saying to them: May God bless you!
And the service of the church continues after this as it should.

F. Service of Holy Communion

This is a symbolic ceremony. It must be performed in a very simple way. The symbols used in the meal must not become an Idol.

The pastor can be helped by the deacons, the elders in the distribution of the elements of communion. The meal can be taken in the Sunday morning or Sunday evening services, or during a separate time.

a. Preparation for the meal.
1. Ensure that the cups, trays, towels are clean.
2. The deacons or elders must be well prepared for their mission.

3. The communion table must be well prepared with all the supplies before the start of the service. The deacons are responsible for the preparation of the table, then the pastor is responsible to check if the table is well prepared.
4. The service before the meal is so members can renew their devotions to the Lord.
5. The service of communion must be announced one week in advance. Some pastors remind members about the service from mouth to ear.
6. In some cases, offerings are collected during the service for the needs of the church.

b. The opening ceremony
   If the service is mixed with baptized members and unbaptized members.
   1. A call is given to the participants. This appeal indicates the qualifications of the people who can participate.
   2. An appropriate song is led by a leader or director of songs. During that time, the participants carry out at the service of washing of the feet (if it is requested) and then they move to receive the elements of communion.
   3. The pastor must choose the passage of Scripture to recite in the breaking of the bread.
   4. Most often people choose the following text: 1 Cor. 11:23-26.
   5. Pray over the elements of communion before distributing them. Sometimes we request a deacon to pray. The pastor must notify the deacon in advance.
   6. After the congregation has been served, an appropriate Scripture can be cited. Then the pastor can proceed with the order of the Lord's Supper.
   7. We can sing a song while deacons and elders collect the cups.
   8. Final Prayer
   9. Blessing.

If the service is not mixed (only baptized members in the service)
   1. The opening of the ceremony.
      Some pastors begin by reading a suitable scripture, such as: Mt. 20.20-30.
   2. Singing in common
      We sing an appropriate hymn.
   3. Invocation prayer

The pastor can do this prayer or his own.

Lord, our God, the God of all eternity, before thee there was no God, after thee there will be none. The God of all grace, who has blessed us with all kinds of spiritual blessings in the heavenly places in Christ! We are once more in thy house to glorify, to exalt, to sing and to participate in the ceremony of remembering the death of your Son, Jesus Christ.

Lord God, we humble ourselves before thee and we ask you to accept us in thy presence. Purify our hearts, wash our body of the sins we have committed. Give us the strength to forgive others who have wounded us. May it be pleasing to you, God, to bless this service, that this service meets its objective to announce the death and the return of the Lord. Receive favorably the words of our lips and the feelings of our hearts. In the name of Jesus Christ, our divine Redeemer, we pray! Amen!

4. If the service is performed with the washing of feet, persons are responsible for directing the assembly in appropriate hymns; and the assembly rises under the orders of those responsible for washing the feet.

5. The message or reflection on the Holy Supper.
The message must appeal to the conscience and to respect for the will of God.

6. The distribution of the elements of the communion.
In large assemblies, we listen to special songs and testimonies while the assembly receives the elements of the communion. In some churches, we adopt the principle that the members move themselves to go take the elements of communion; in other churches the deacons distribute.

7. The Lord's Supper
Some pastors adopt the practice of reading 1 Cor. 11.23-29 before taking the meal, and they grant a time of reflection to the participants in the sermon. Others adopt the practice of proceeding with the meal. Whatever the practice adopted, the pastor can make a short prayer before taking the meal. Then, the pastor, raising the right hand and taking the bread says: For I have received from the lord that which also I delivered unto you, that the Lord Jesus the same night in which he was betrayed took bread: and when he had given thanks, he broke it, and said, take, eat; this is my body, which is broken for you; this do in remembrance of me. Eat together.

After a few seconds, the pastor says: After the same manner, also he took the cup, when he had supped, saying, this cup is the new testament in my blood: this do you as oft as you drink it, in remembrance of me. Drink together.

8. Song of closure

    After Christians have finished taking the meal, the celebrant says a word of thanks. Then he invites the congregation to stand to sing a hymn with him, while the officers collect the cups. It is suitable to sing a hymn of joy, of hope, of consecration or forgiveness.

9. Final prayer

    This must take account of the grace of God and the sacrifice of Jesus. Here is a model:

    Blessed be the God and Father of Our Lord Jesus Christ, who loves us, who delivered us from our sins by his blood, and who has made us a kingdom, priests to God his Father. Thank you for the sacrifice of Jesus, your only Son, because it is impossible that the blood of bulls and goats remove sins. Thank you also for this service which reminds us of the death and resurrection of Jesus Christ. Give us, God, the strength to walk with Christ for always, and that we are witnesses for him and ambassadors. This is the prayer that we address, by Jesus Christ, our divine Redeemer. Amen!

10. Blessing

    "The God of peace, who brought back from the dead the great Shepherd of the sheep, by the blood of the eternal covenant, our Lord Jesus, make you capable of any good work for the fulfilment of its faith that is in you, that is pleasing to him, through Jesus Christ, to whom be glory to the centuries of the centuries! Amen!"

Always working, and do not faint.

13

MARRIAGE DEPARTMENT

A. The laws of marriage

1. Who can be married?
    In its legal sense, marriage is the union of two persons contracted with the conditions required from one another. The religious definition of marriage is an alliance agreement between two persons of the opposite sex to procreate, and in view of perpetuating society.

    These two definitions can establish a difference between a contract of marriage and an alliance of marriage, or between a religious and a civil marriage. The first is done in the court house by a judge, which receives its power from the state, while the second receives its power from God. On the other hand, the contract of marriage is based on the mutual respect of the contract while the alliance is based on love. Therefore, it is recommended to our singles to have their marriages performed by a religious minister.

2. Conditions at the marriage
    The religious minister may refuse a marriage in advance without these conditions.

    a. The difference in sex.
        The Bible, the only reliable document in matters of faith, recognizes the marriage between a man and a woman. A man leaves his father and his mother and is joined to his wife. (Gen. 2.24).

    b. The age

The marriageable age varies according to the law of the country or the region in major countries such as the United States.

c. The consent of the future spouses

It is an indispensable condition to the marriage. The consent of the parents in the case of minors; it is necessary to check if the consent paper respects the legal view.

d. The medical examination

Some countries recommend a medical examination before marriage.

B. The Marriage Service

The religious minister performs a marriage as an officer of the State and the Church.

He must know the laws relating to the environment. The mayor of the city can help in this direction.

1. Before the service
   a. The minister must be sure that he meets all legal conditions according to the law to celebrate a marriage.
   b. If the minister has any doubts about the marriage, it would be good to contact the elders of the church in this matter.
   c. The religious minister must examine the documents of the marriage:
      1. The authorization of the marriage -- is it legal?
      2. The date has not expired?
      3. If the medical examination is recommended, is it normal?
      4. None of the future spouses has had a previous marriage?
   d. Prenuptial counsel
      1. The counseling is free of charge.
      2. Some pastors do a ceremony practice before the day of the wedding.
      3. The most important
         - Compatibility, the couple living with family members.
         - The work after the marriage.
         - -How to raise the children.
         - The objectives in life of the future spouses.
         - Spirituality, family devotion.

- The seriousness of marriage, the requirements of conjugal life in the home.
- The spouses and the community know the problems for Christians evolving in their community.
- Precautions against prenuptial relations.
- The marriage between a believer and a non-believer or an opposite doctrine is not desirable because their hopes are different.
- Practice for the service of marriage and the reception

The pastor can skip this step if the ceremony will take place at the house and the future spouses are old.

a. Determine with the future spouses the decoration of the temple and the magnitude of the ceremony, the punctuality and the duration of the service.

b. The reception
   Some religious ministers do not judge it necessary to participate.

c. The ushers must match the magnitude of their task.

2. During the service of marriage.

a. The celebrant must follow all the suggestions of the bride concerning decorations, directions, music, etc. He must avoid any other counsel from a member of the family.

b. The celebrant must be obedient to the laws of the service.

c. He must register marriages with the names, places, dates.

d. The celebrant must work to remember all the details of this service, because there are so many things to do and they must go exactly as planned.

e. The wedding procession
   For the procession, a wedding planner or a manual can help the spouses to make their procession choice. While the parents and the guests take their seats, the officiating clergy invites the future spouses and participants to turn to him. And the ceremony begins.
   It is necessary to arrange to have someone to receive the carrier of the ring during the ceremony.

The opening of the ceremony

There is no absolute rule. But according to the magnitude of the ceremony, it is good to have an appropriate standard. A manual can help the officiant with this subject. I will propose a way to proceed.

When everything is in place, the officiating clergy shall remind everyone concerned to turn their faces toward him if they were turned toward the assembly. Then the officiant can begin as well:

Ladies and gentlemen, we have been invited here today to the marriage of Mr.................................. and Miss............................ They are going in a few moments to share their wishes and their consents. (Some places, we must make a last publication of marriage: if someone knows some just impediment why Mr. ....and Miss...................... cannot unite in the marriage, let him say so now or in the future he remains silent).

Mr. .... and Miss............................ you come to this sanctuary to unite in the bonds of marriage. The union of the man and the woman was instituted by God himself. It is a solemn manner that today you are going to declare before your witnesses, your parents and these guests that you will live as husband and wife in the love and tenderness that you share. You will discover that you have become only one flesh in the communion of your thoughts, in your aspirations, and children that you will have. Know that God is the first witness of the act that you are going to perform today.

Opening song
Invocation prayer
Scripture reading
Organ or vocal music
A short sermon
Special music

Questions on the commitment of the future spouses:

- The officiant invites the spouses and the witnesses to stand.
- Addressing the groom, Mr..................., do you want to take Miss............... here present, for your lawful wife?

Groom: I want with all my heart.

- Promise to the love, cherish, protect and to remain faithful to her as long as you both live?

Groom: Yes, I promise.

- Speaking to the Bride, Miss................, do you want to take Mr. ....here present, to be your lawful husband?

Bride: I want with all my heart.

- Promise to love, cherish, honor, and obey him and to remain faithful to him as long as you both live?

Bride: Yes, I promise.

Exchanges of Vows:

The officiant says: Given that Mr. .... and Miss .... responded affirmatively to the question if they want to take each other as spouses. We ask Mr. .... turn to Miss .... (taking her right hand) and repeat after me (the celebrant reads his paper if he has not memorized it) I, ... take unto thee.....................for my lawful wife. I promise to love and to live with you today and to keep thee near me, to give thee all my affection, honor and respect you, and to share with you the grace of my God.

Still hand in hand, the bride watching her groom, repeats the same words.

Then the celebrant takes the rings and presents them to the spouses and witnesses, saying:

These rings are circles symbolizing no beginning or end. It is the symbol of Infinity and eternity. These rings are the sign that you agree to respect each other, the links that unite you today the one to the other.

On the commitment of the future spouses.

Speaking to the man, the celebrant offers the first ring, asking him to repeat after him: I give you this ring as a pledge of the love that I have for you and the respect of the link that unites me to thee forever (the husband puts the ring to the fourth finger of the left hand of the wife).

Speaking to the woman, the celebrant offers the other ring to the bride, asking her to repeat after him the same words and place the ring on the same finger of her husband.

Prayer of Consecration

Special music plays as the celebrant asks the husband and the wife to kneel down for the prayer of consecration.

The celebrant can do this prayer or his own:

God of the universe, the Creator of heaven and earth, the Redeemer of sinful man, author of everything excellent and every perfect gift, we present to you, Lord now, it is to consecrate this couple to you. This couple is before thee, we beseech thee to grant them your strength, help them to succeed in the act they have just done. Lord, we ask you to give the rain of the first and the rear season so that they can live together in peace, fidelity, joy, and love, and that their marriage be crowned with success. Help them, Lord God, to have the mutual support to be able to share the good times and the bad. Spread on them faith, hope and love so their home can survive the difficulties inherent in married life. Grant them support for the success of their life. We are asking you all these graces in the name of Jesus, your only Son, to whom is the glory and honor to the centuries of the centuries. Amen!

The spouses join hands and look at each other. The celebrant says: Mr.................and Miss................... you consent in the presence of God, and all this assembly, to join you in the bonds of marriage and you have made a demonstration of alliance in giving and receiving a ring each. Under the authority given to me as a minister of God, I declare you husband and wife. May God bless you and make you happy.

Now we ask Mr..............to lift the veil (if there is one) to embrace his wife.

Presentation of the new couple to the assembly.

Ladies and gentlemen,

I have the honor to present to you this new couple, Mr. and Mrs................... You can applaud them.

The signature of the act of marriage.
The spouses and the witnesses are invited to move to affix their signature to the act of marriage.

Benediction
May God Almighty, all loving and all good, turn his face toward you and make you full of his grace, that he fills you with his love, that he makes you and your home a source of joy, peace and happiness, now and for-ever. Amen!

Extra formalities ceremonial:

a. The ushers clear the auditorium.
b. If the minister goes to the reception, he should bring a gift for the couple.
c. In case the minister must submit a certificate of marriage, he must return it to the woman.
d. Daily devotions for the first week of the marriage; the minister may create a sheet with portions of the writing, prayers and poems for each day.
e. Recommendations for the husbands and wives. Examples for the husbands: Thou shalt not to praise the food of thy mother in the presence of your wife. Honor your mother-in-law. Examples for women: thou shalt have no other man beside thy husband, you must respect your husband.
f. The couple must fight against bad attitudes (selfish, inputs and outputs) etc.
g. The couple promises to dedicate their lives and their home to Christ and to his service. Please turn regularly to divine counsel in the planning for the home. Read the Word daily to know the will of God, to present fairly the services of the Church, to practice the teachings of Christ to the house (Joshua 24:15)
h. Revision of prenuptial promises such as: Church of affiliation, objectives, plans, commitment, number of children desired, etc.
i. A letter of congratulation can be addressed to the couple containing: the announcement of marriage and the congratulation, Bible reading, invitation to new couple to the services of the Church. A small poem may accompany it, and then the signature.

May the marriage be honored by all!

14

FUNERALS DEPARTMENT

A funeral service is one of the most difficult services that the minister of God is called to lead. However, it is a great opportunity to comfort the relatives and friends, the people who came for a last tribute to the memory of the dead, and to bring the blessing of faith. The service must be well prepared and very comforting. People sometimes want to rethink their spiritual lives because of this departure. In this moment, it is necessary to demonstrate the magnitude of Christian love.

Protestant churches do not pray for the dead. The funeral service is addressed to the living, because the Word says: *It is reserved for men to die once* (Heb. 9.27). Therefore, the fate of the dead is already decided, the service is not a service in favor of the dead.

It is not necessary for an ordained minister to lead a funeral service. However, the celebrant must pay close attention to this service he is called to preside over, because it will be directed to an audience composed of different layers of society, believers and unbelievers, believers who are weak in faith, and atheists. For this reason, this service must be well prepared. The celebrant should not make any reference to the cause of death, to avoid any distracting elements. The preacher must proclaim the Word of God and not the life of the dead, because sometimes people in the audience know better than the preacher.

A few lines of tips for a funeral service.

A. Before the funeral.

1. After having received the news, the minister goes to the house of the dead. He offers sympathy and help. If possible, he prays with the family.
2. During the day or the day after, he goes to the dead person's house to arrange the services. He must remind the family that he is there to carry out their will and not to impose anything.

B. The service at the church.

1. The celebrant must be at the church at least fifteen minutes before the beginning of the service. This allows him to have enough time to properly organize himself.
2. In some cases, the coffin is open for the service, in others the casket is closed before proceeding to the service. In any event, after the preliminary music, the celebrant will rise from his seat and take his place to begin the service. In some traditions, the attendees will shake hands with the members of the family before taking their places.
3. The celebrant must avoid rushing the service.
4. Opening of the ceremony.
   The celebrant chooses an opening statement, such as: Dear brothers and sisters and friends, the peace of the Lord rest on you all! We are here in this sanctuary for a last tribute to the memory of.......... who is dead. We are still alive. This is the time for us to enjoy life and the author of life, God. We are therefore going to thank and praise him once again for this grace.
5. Scripture reading.
   Choose an appropriate text such as: Jn 14; Ps 23; 90; 103; Rom. 8; I Thess. 4, or consult a manual.
6. Singing in common.
   There is a whole series of songs collected for such a circumstance.
7. Invocation prayer.
   Exalt the name of God, including the grace and goodness of God and implore the favor of God for the service.
8. Obituary (if it is recommended).
   a. The full name of the dead.
   b. Date and place of birth
   c. Parents.
   d. His education, if it is honorable.

  e. Children, spouse and their housing environment.

  f. The work accomplished by the dead in his life.

9. Presentation of condolences.

10. Message

The message should be provided to help the living, especially if the dead was a Christian. If the person was not a Christian, the celebrant does not need to mention his or her eternal state. The sermon must be evangelical, but will not make a direct call to salvation. The officiant must avoid exerting pressure on the family or friends of the dead.

11. A little music, if it is recommended.

12. Prayer of consolation.

This must be addressed to the name of the parents, spouse and children, siblings, other relatives, friends and allies, and it must aim to seek the divine energy for these affected people.

13. Benediction

To the one who can protect you in any fall, and make you appear before his glory irreproachable and in joy, to God alone, our Savior, through Jesus Christ our Lord, be glory, majesty, strength and power, and now and forever, in all the centuries! Amen!

14. Now whatever the formula used, the religious group must be ready to minister any aid to ease any signs of distress among the mourners.

15. Now, the minister should avoid going to the cemetery in the company of family, and should keep a respectful silence and should not joke with anyone. At the cemetery, wait until the casket has arrived at the gravesite and that the coffin is well placed before proceeding to the service of the cemetery.

C. At the cemetery

Sometimes the pastor does not accompany the procession to the cemetery. In this case, a skilled leader must lead this service. Most often, this ceremony is brief, especially if it is cold.

1. The opening of the ceremony

The celebrant intones one or two stanzas of an appropriate hymn.

2. Reading of the Word

He chooses a very short reading that he has prepared in advance.

3. Singing in common (if possible)

Sometimes a song is sung during the burial. Other times, proceed directly to the burial.

4. Formula of burial.

It is recommended to be informed of the custom of the community. Sometimes according to the custom, a shovel of earth is placed on the coffin by the funeral director. In some places, rose petals are scattered, in others three pinches of earth. When the body has been deposited in the tomb, the celebrant steps to the front and says: "The dust will return to the earth as it was, and the spirit will return to God who gave it" (Eccl.12.7).

5. Final prayer

A short prayer is addressed to God, showing the power of God, the need for consolation for the members of the family of the dead. I always like to finish these prayers with the Lord's Prayer: "Our Father... "

6. Benediction

The God of peace brings you his peace, by Jesus Christ, our divine Savior. Amen!

7. A few useful tips.

The celebrant must pay attention to the place where he will stand in front of the family to officiate the service. He must be sure where he is going to stand is safe enough.

D. After the funeral.

1. Keep a good registry of burials with the names, dates, locations and ages.

2. The pastor can visit the family of the dead a few days after the funeral.

There is a time for everything.

15

FINANCES DEPARTMENT

A. Collection of Funds

The church is responsible before God for the wise use of the money that it receives. The pastor must be well equipped financially to guide the people in the collection, recording and reporting the funds of the church. He must encourage the faithful to contribute in the work of God." .... for God loves a cheerful giver "(2 Cor. 9.7).

1. General principles.
   a. The pastor must know that God is the master of any material thing without excluding the money.
   b. Man is a simple administrator and user of material things.
   c. Man must give a report of everything that is under his control.
   d. The love of money is the root of all evils. My beloved, our lives are dedicated to the Lord, including our love.
   e. Christians must give and use their money to create a Christian character.
   f. The church must avoid the greed that makes war on the soul.
   g. The church must keep an accurate report.
   h. The needs of the church must be presented to the congregation.
   i. Man looks to what strikes the eyes, what he can see.
   j. The pastor must pray for the donors and their money.
   k. The pastor or the leaders, in educating the new members on their obligations toward the church, must include the financial obligations. We must teach tithing to the church.

l.   The pastor must convince the people that the money they give is used wisely.

m.   The money collected must be spent only for the affairs of the church.

2.   Ways to collect funds for the church

Tithes

The tithe is the tenth part of your income, what you have been given (Gen. 28.22). This part belongs to God (Lev. 27.30). Abraham was the first to pay the tithe to Melchizedek (Gen. 14.20). Then Jacob in Gen. 28.20-22. And the scribes and the Pharisees Mt. 23.23

a.   Where should we pay the tithe?
The tithe is for the house of God (Mal. 3.10). As well it must be paid to the place where you receive spiritual blessing. Examples: Gen. 26.12; 1 Cor. 9.11

b.   The reasons for the payment of the tithe.
1.   It is a commandment of God, Lev. 27.30
2.   It is a form of worship or of obedience, Gen. 14.18-20
3.   So that there is food in the house of God, Lev. 3:10; Num. 18; 20-31
4.   It is recognition that God is the source of any income, Ps 50.10-13.
5.   Because Jesus asks us not to neglect doing so, Mt. 23.23.

c.   The benefits of paying the tithe.
1.   The donor will escape the punishment of God, Lev. 3.11
2.   There is blessing in abundance for the donor, Mal. 3.10
3.   The devourer will be hunted, Lev. 3.11
4.   The donor will become a source of blessing and joy, Lev. 3.12
5.   The donor receives a double blessing (spiritual and material), Lev. 3.7-10.

The offerings

These are gifts that we offer to God. They must be of value. 2 Sam. 24.24. It is a voluntary donation. The offering also includes the vows and gages. Ezra 1.4.

Vows

A vow is a promise made to God to give or do something in return for what he has done for us, 1 Sam. 1.11. The vows are irrevocable, Num. 30.3. The cessation of payment of vows involve disastrous consequences, Eccl. 5.4-5.

Gages

The gages are freewill offerings made to God for a specific need in the ministry, Neh. 7.70-72

   a.   The principles involved in the offering
     1.   It must be desired or voluntary, 2 Cor. 8.12; Num.25.1.
     2.   It must agree with the ability of the donor, 2 Cor. 8.1, 2.
     3.   It must be made with joy, 2 Cor. 9.7
   b.   The blessings that include the offering

You receive to the same extent that you have given, Luke 6.38; 2 Cor. 9.6
   c.   The plan for each member
     1.   Each house is visited by an official member of the church with the objective of encouraging attendance and support of the church.
     2.   The individual questions relating to the budget of the church are answered in each house.
     3.   The members are united in a common purpose.
     4.   The church thrives both spiritually and financially.

F. Registry of finance of the church

It is important to keep an adequate financial register. The church can use modern technologies to save the financial data to help the congregation as needed. After each service, it must save the data:

1.   Offerings in the envelopes.
2.   Offerings without envelopes.
3.   Special gifts.
4.   Offerings for missionaries.
5.   All other offerings received.

If there is an expenditure, it must be mentioned, such as:
   a.   Mortgage costs.
   b.   The items of the budget.
   c.   The unexpected fees.
   d.   All other expenditures.

Data must be recorded accurately to be able to give a clear monthly report. This monthly report will be threefold: a copy for the pastor, another for the responsible members of the administration, and a copy for the treasurer.

This financial report of the church, the financial status of the church, must be clear to the members. It must be updated weekly.

G. Report model
1. Beginning of cash.
2. Amount received.
3. Expenditures.
4. New totals.

The items will be carried over to the current fund, building funds, investment funds, missionary funds, funds for electricity, etc.

H. Budget of the Church
In the adequate situation, the church must have an annual budget, and this budget must be published so all members may have knowledge and know progress is being made regarding this budget.

1. The budget of the church is drawn up by a committee composed of all the major organizations of the church, with the committee of the administration, and this budget must include:
   a. Sunday School department.
   b. Music department.
   c. Women's department.
   d. Youth department
   e. Children's department
   f. Evangelism department
2. Some churches submit the budget for a vote of the assembly.
3. We must establish the date of the commencement of the budget. Most often, the budget starts on January 1 and ends on December 31.
4. In the case of votes
   The budget committee must have this budget ready before the date of the vote.
5. The expenditure of the budget
   More often:
   a. Wages
   b. Management of the property
   c. Educational materials
   d. Programs
   e. Secretary
   f. Members

    g.   Workers
    h.   Prayer committee
    i.   Missionary budget
    j.   Diverse fees
    k.   Total

"Who serves as a soldier at his own expense? "(1 Cor.9.7).

I. Formation in Organization

1. This formation must encompass from the young people of the church up to the more mature, in all departments. The Sunday school is very important in this area of Christian education.
2. The Sunday school can use modern means (films, visual aids) to show the responsibilities of the organization.
3. The Sunday school may encourage responsibility on the part of students and teachers to make the offering time full of adoration and significance. We can share one or a few verses at this time to show the biblical emphasis.
4. Education in the organization should include training on tithing.
5. The organization will be considered important if it is not interested only in the collection of funds, but also in using talents and other important things.
6. There are places where one can find materials of organization. We must not neglect them.

Let us be good stewards of the various graces of God.

16

THE PASTOR AND THE CHURCH BUSINESS MEETING

The business meeting is a meeting that is of great importance, to give the reports of the activities of the church and to assist the church to stay true to its calling Sometimes the meeting is chaired by the pastor, other times by a person chosen according to the principles of the church. The business meeting must bring together the largest number of people possible. To achieve this, it is necessary to use appropriate methods to make the announcement of the meeting.

A. The Meeting
1. Agenda
    a. Invitation to come to order
    b. Prayer
    c. Reading of the minutes of the last meeting
    d. Acceptance of these minutes
    e. Former subjects
    f. New topics
    g. Adjournments
    h. Prayer
2. General principles of the meeting
    a. The pastor must be open to discussions
    b. The pastor must be open to the vote if it is necessary.
    c. The pastor must demonstrate humility, i.e., compromise where it is necessary.

d. Keep a complete record of transactions. Arrange a table for the Secretary.

e. There must be an established time for the meeting.

f. Prepare the agenda well before the meeting. If possible, communicate the agenda in advance to the members.

g. Seek the counsel of God for the meeting. Have prayers at the beginning of the meeting.

h. Read the agenda at the time provided during the meeting.

i. There is a need to focus on the immediate affairs.

j. Ask the members if there are unclear points and listen to their points of view.

k. In the case where the points of view would be shared, take time for this before proceeding to the vote.

l. It is good to classify subjects of the same type together to save time.

m. You must leave room to address issues of general interest.

n. The date of the next meeting.

J. Annual Report of the Church.

1. The annual report must be prepared by all departments of the church. Each department must send its report in the time provided to the office of the church to enable the secretary to have time to organize and to make the necessary copies. Each department must ensure that its report is accurate, because it will be open to discussion.

2. Estimate the length and the importance of each element of the report.

3. The order of the elements of the annual report.

    a. The officers of the church.

    b. The commissions of the church.

    c. The departments of the church.

A harsh word stirs up anger.

17

Church Planting

There is not an accurate method of church planting. Church planting is always done following a vision, an idea that we have, and the ways and means available.

A. The Department of Church Planting
The term Church Planter is the modern version of the old concept of "Pioneer."

Some specificities of this department.
1. Be called to this service
   The traveler of the Lord said in 1 Cor. 9.16," For if I preach the gospel, I have nothing to boast of, for necessity is laid upon me; yes, woe is me if I do not preach the gospel." Any effective work of God is done by vocation. The department of church planting requires the meeting of three departments: evangelism, building, and the structuring of the church. Therefore, the training of an evangelist is not sufficient only for this work, he must be a pastor-evangelist. This work was done in the early church by the apostles. In Rom. 15.20, the Apostle Paul tells us:" I have made it my aim to preach the gospel, not where Christ was named, lest I should build on another man's foundation."

2. The courage of the service
   The call to itself is not enough, we must have the courage. The LORD said to Joshua, Josh. 1.6, he must have the courage for the conquest of the land of Canaan. The same for the conquest of souls, we need courage. This explains a zeal, a dynamism capable

of working a vision, to establish the steps to success with the help of God. This courage requires strict discipline and a spirit of essential genius.

3. The training for the service
   According to 2 Cor. 3.6, the Apostle Paul tells us:" God has made us able to be ministers." As was pointed out by Pastor Reinhard Bonnke, of *Christ For All Nations*, "the sign of the living Christ is an empty tomb, not an empty church"[18]. To fill the church, the disciples had to train first; three years at the foot of the Master, ten days in the Upper Room. They were formed before the descent of the Holy Spirit on them. The Apostle Paul had to spend three years in Saudi or at least in the desert of Arabia. The theologians affirm that he went there to form himself. The Lord Jesus chose Paul to carry the Gospel before the greats, he had to be a well-prepared minister. In this third millennium, knowledge increases so that the people who are listening to us are more educated than the time of Paul. The lack of knowledge is not going to kill you in one coup, he will end up by killing you if you are still in the same condition, because the Bible says in Hos. 4.6, "My people perish for lack of knowledge." You must be determined to learn, to reflect, to develop the knowledge theologically and socially. To succeed well in this department, you must have knowledge and a discernment of this world. As leader of the kingdom of light, you must seek the light. In Proverbs 4.7, the word teaches us to buy wisdom.

K. The Characteristics of Church Planter.

1. Passion for the lost.
   The apostle told us in Rom. 15.20:" I have made my aim to preach the gospel, not where Christ was named..." The New Living Translation uses the word "ambition," a holy ambition to announce to the lost their God, their Savior. An ambition to banish the blindness of the lost. The apostle continues to say in 1 Tim. 2:3-4, "This is good, and pleases God our Savior, who wants all men to be saved and to come to the knowledge of the truth."

---

[18] Reinhard Bonnke, *Evangelism by Fire,* page 125.

2. The principle of the Kingdom.
   Identify the brothers. You have not gone in a place for a war of denominations. On the contrary, you must visit the other pastors of the other churches and talk to them about your projects.

3. A visionary.
   Where there is no vision, the people cast off restraint... (Proverbs 29.18). A church planter must be a visionary. This means that he needs a vision from God. He must wait for God like the disciples who remained in Jerusalem until the day of Pentecost. The prophecy was fulfilled in them and they received their visions.

4. A love for the people.
   Allow me to quote the great Scottish church planter, David Livingstone, in his journal: "We are like voices crying in the wilderness; we prepare the way for a glorious future. Future missionaries will be rewarded with conversions for every sermon. We are their pioneers and helpers.
   "Let them not forget the watchman of the night -- us who worked when all was gloom, and no evidence of success in the way of conversion cheered our paths. They will doubtless have more light than we; but we can serve our Master earnestly and proclaim the Gospel as they will do."
   A person may not work as an effective church planter without being pushed by the love of God and being of good heart.

Paul says:

As we have been approved by God to be entrusted with the gospel, even so we speak, not as pleasing men, but God who tests our heart (1 Thessalonians 2.4)

5. The willingness to sacrifice.
   The work of church planting is a call to sacrifice. "Don't give up; the beginning is always the hardest" (Kemmy Nola). Sometimes, the financial sacrifice is enormous until the church is established. The Apostle Paul said, for though I am free from all, I have made myself a servant to all, that I might win more of them (1 Cor. 9.19).

6. Support of the family

   The growers of churches are not angels, they are tempted daily like the whole world. Therefore, the physical and emotional relationships of marriage are important for the new babies in the faith. The family of the minister must be a model for the new converted, so that they can see the new life in Christ. I think that it is in this sense that Paul, in his first epistle to Timothy said: if anyone aspires to the office of overseer, he desires a noble task. Therefore, an overseer must be above reproach, the husband of one wife, sober-minded, self-controlled, respectable, hospitable, able to teach, not a drunkard, not violent but gentle, not quarrelsome, not a lover of money. He must manage his own household well, with all dignity keeping his children submissive (1 Tim. 3.1-5).

7. The leader or the servant.

   "Leaders have a significant role in creating the state of mind that is the society. They can serve as symbols of the moral unity of the society. They can express the values that hold the society together. Most important, they can conceive and articulate goals that lift people out of their petty preoccupations, carry them above conflicts that tear a society apart, and unite them in pursuit of objectives worthy of their best efforts".[19]

   The people are always in search of a leader in any society. The leader must have a voluntary attitude and not of coercion, motivated not by a personal interest but by a spirit of service, conduct by example and not by force. The Apostle Peter exhorts us in this sense: Like Shepherdstown the flock of God among you. Watch over it. Don't shepherd because you must, but do it voluntarily for God. Don't shepherd greedily, but do it eagerly (1 Pet. 5.2)

L. Seven steps Toward the Establishment of a Church.

The "seven stages" to which we are referring are those developed in the brochure, "Seven Steps to the Implementation of a Church." It presents the steps by which the apostle Paul will pass when he is going to establish the church of Philippi. (Acts 16.9-15) This approach is not just a strategy for planting a church, it also provides a more holistic view of things.

---

[19] Bennis & Nanus, *Leaders*, page 200.

Step 1: God gives a vision

In Acts 16, the Bible tells us that the apostle Paul had reached the city of Troas, which was for him the last city in Asia where missionaries could preach the good news. God attracted Paul's attention by a vision: a Macedonian appeared to him, and prayed to him: "Go to Macedonia, help us!"

Vision is the first step in the establishment of a new church. Vision captivates a person and gives him a sense of authority. Vision is not defined by what the person wants to do, or even where the person wants to go. Instead, the vision is how God helps a person create as "a mental picture, a picture," of what he expects from his servant.

Paul's vision was so specific that the nationality of man in the vision was revealed to him. Paul no longer relied on his own reason: "Let us return to the brethren in all the cities where we have spoken the word of the Lord, to see in what state they are." (Acts 15.36) There was a new sense of authority in Paul's plans.

(Acts 15.36b) From this moment, Paul will follow God's agenda, not his desire to "return to the brothers."

The following list of steps will help the local church team prepare for a new congregation. The different teams involved in the implementation will have a challenge: to define their vision and to develop a support system for the new nascent church. These same teams will also be able to seek partnerships to benefit from all the resources available to them.

Steps to be taken (specify the expected start date, date and completion date)

1.1 Receiving a vision from God about the new church.

1.2 Plan on a Sunday morning commitment to the establishment of a new church.

1.3 Develop an intercession prayer plan for the establishment of churches.

1.4 Engage partners in ministries who feel God's call to participate in the establishment of a new church.

1.5 Consult and initiate a partnership with the Mission Director and the new project team (also, known as the Mission Development Board).

1.6 Consult with the church missionary(s) in the area concerned for help in identifying a target community for the new church, and potential candidates for the beginning.

1.7 Develop the vision of the new church by considering patterns of church planting.

1.8 Define the target community / target group; Collect data by conducting a demographic study.

1.9 Join a multiplication network of churches.

Cooperative relations
1. The local church
2. A missionary in a regional church establishment
3. The Regional Convention
4. Other denominations that would like to join and commit to helping the new church

Step 2: Form a team
The Bible suggests that the first actions of the Apostle Paul were to communicate the vision he had received from God to the other members of the missionary team. The Bible tells us: "We immediately sought to go to Macedonia, concluding that the Lord was calling us to announce the good news." (Acts 16.10)

When a church planter works alone, the number of people and Bible study groups he can influence is restricted! Only one member of the team can be able to do everything alone: conduct the service of praise and preach a sermon. On the other hand, a congregation, by definition, has several functions: the study of the Bible, praise, evangelization, fraternal communion, ministry, multiplication of disciples, and missions. A single church planter cannot fulfill these functions with the same efficiency as a team could do.

It takes the effort of a whole team for the proper functioning of a congregation. The Bible does not give us a definite description of all the members of the team who traveled with Paul, but Silas was identified as part of the healing ministry. Silas was in prison with Paul after the young woman who was following them was cured of demonic possession.

The "we" of Acts 16.10 must be recognized by the churches as a model to follow when they consider the implantation of a new church. We must find people who are "gifted": natural talent(s) and spiritual gift(s) to fulfill the various functions required by the new congregation.

The following approaches and resources will assist churches in recruiting people for the settlement team.

Steps to be taken (specify the expected start date, date and completion date)

2.1 Identify and hire a church planter. This one could be a person in your own church!

2.2 Build a support system for the church planter: Husband, mentor, supervisor, intercession team.

2.3 Identify and engage people (apostolic persons) who wish to be part of a new church.

2.4 Clarify functions - praise, biblical study, communion, etc. - and enlist a team.

2.5 Enlisting servants for the ministry of children.

2.6 Confirm your announced partnerships Chapter 1: individuals, churches, local association, regional convention and others.

2.7 Suggest that the church planter build a network of relationships for ongoing support.

Step 3: From a vision to a place

The Bible tells us: "We immediately sought to go to Macedonia ..." (Acts 16.10) Paul's vision of the Macedonian pushed the missionary team to act immediately. The boat on which they embarked stopped at Samothrace, then at Neapolis, and finally at Philippi, which the Bible calls "the first city of a Macedonian district." The boat did not take them directly to Philippi. There were several ports to cross along the way.

It is sometimes necessary to cross several ports before the vision of planting a church is fulfilled. The establishment of a church often requires a plan, also called a prospectus. This plan is drawn from the vision and will outline how to start the new congregation.

"The place" mentioned in this section can be a geographical area as was the case for the city of Philippi. It may also designate a group of individuals as it was for the Macedonians. The whole question of "the place" will be developed more fully during the development of the site plan.

The following steps will be useful in developing a coherent plan.

Steps to be followed (specify opposite the start date, and the expected completion date)

3.1 Further Develop Your Mission:

Mission Statement and Statement of Faith
Biblical and Spiritual Foundations
Values
Annual Goals

3.2 Writing a proposal for church planting

3.3 Describe and develop a ministry development group

3.4 Creating Conventions:
Completing Partnerships
Developing the Convention for the New Church

3.5 Develop a strategy like that of the early churches
Work on the plan for the new church
Make a "brain-storming" meeting with the benchmarking team.

3.6 Seek out the place God chose for the new church and identify a potential place for encounters.

3.7 Developing a Budget:
Estimate the income for the first year.
Secure resources for the new church.

3.8 Develop a plan for public relations.

3.9 Choose a name for the church and confirm the mailing address.

Step 4: Find Receptive People

The search for receptive people in Acts 16 tells us the story of the first Sabbath day in Philippi for the church planting team. "On the Sabbath, we went out of the gate to a river where we thought there was (a place of) prayer." (Acts 16.13)

There is no doubt that Paul was looking for receptive people in the cities where the missionary team had implanted new congregations. In Asia, the missionary team sought receptive people in the synagogues. "In Iconium, Paul and Barnabas also entered the synagogue of the Jews." (Acts 14.1) The missionary team turned to the Jews and the Gentiles who had the fear of the Lord, to find receptive minds among them.

The first form of receptivity needed by the church planting team is an introduction to the community or target group. This introduction is most effective when it comes from a respected member of the community itself. Church planters of the past call this person "the person of peace." This person may be a member of a religious community. These "people of peace" will often be sympathetic to the implants of a new congregation and will likely become friends of the settlement team. On the other hand, they are not always candidates for the church they help to promote.

The second form of receptivity is to the potential members of the new church. God always guides a settlement team to a community or group of people where he has prepared resource persons for the launch of the new church. The following steps will help the different implantation teams in their search for receptive people.

Steps (specify the start date, and the expected completion date)

4.1 Verify the results of demographic studies by conducting surveys in the community

4.2 Begin to cultivate the community
    Identify the first candidates
    Enter the key community networks
    Have an interview with the key people in the community

4.3 Begin Bible studies of evangelism

4.4 Establish an assimilation system

4.5 Determine the initial organization of the church and the decision-making processes

Step 5: Evangelize the unbelievers

Evangelizing the Unbelievers

Receptivity is confirmed by seeing people professing faith in Jesus Christ as their Savior. The Bible tells us: "One of them, named Lydia, [...] a woman fearing God was listening, and the Lord opened her heart to be attentive to what Paul said." (Acts 16.14)

The evangelization of non-believers is at the heart of the task God has assigned to today's church, as Jesus said: "I am with you every day, even unto the end of the world. "(Mt. 28.20) The church of each new generation is responsible for the responsibility of joining its society. The question is: "How?" and not "If ..." This is the question that should be asked by each church planting team: How should we go about evangelizing?

Evangelization must be intentional. It will not take place if there are no plans to use the different tools and methodologies available. The church planting team should be prepared to use several approaches to evangelism.

It may have a preferred "style," but this one will not necessarily work for all members. Examples of evangelistic approaches: personal evangelism, media, ministry, prayer, sports and public events.

If the team uses only one method of evangelism, the witnesses of the congregation will not be adequately trained.

The following steps may help the Church Implementation Team and / or Mission Team in the church to involve each member in evangelism.

Steps to be completed (specify opposite the start date, and the expected completion date)

5.1 Develop a prayer plan for the new church

5.2 Continue to perform prayer marches in the target community.

5.3 Adopt a plan of evangelization, identify the different methods possible.

5.4 Equip participants with evangelistic methods.

5.5 Select the date for a ministry in the target community.

5.6 Increase evangelistic efforts in the target community:
   By making many phone calls
   "Acts of Kindness" as evangelistic projects
   Special events of evangelization

5.7 Have a pre-launch activity a few weeks before the celebration (Great Opening) of the launch of the new church.

5.8 Begin developing ideas and plans for breeding leaders and churches.

5.9 Discover the core members.

Step 6: Form a core

The core is an extension of the church planting team. As a new believer, Lydia invited the Paul-led settlement team to enter her house (Acts 16.15), and the Bible tells us that she persuaded them. She immediately joined the task already begun by the implementation team.

The development process begins when a new convert joins the implementation team as a member of the kernel. In their book, **Connecting**, Paul D. Stanley and J. Robert Clinton define the process of multiplying disciples as "a relational process in which an experienced disciple of Christ shares with a new believer commitment, understanding, and as the skills necessary to know and obey Jesus Christ as His Savior."

The nuclei that are the results of evangelistic efforts need time to discover the novelty of this life in Christ. They also need time to enter communion with other believers. One of the essential responsibilities of the church planting team, following an evangelistic event, is to make disciples of new believers and provide them with an environment where they will be safe for the first steps of their growth to be done properly.

The members of the nucleus must go further than the needs of fraternal communion and formation. The mission team must be able to rethink the vision of church planting with the core members. A Mission spokesperson is responsible to both the church planting team and the nucleus for a historical and spiritual account of the need for a new church.

The following steps will help the Church Implementation Team and / or Mission Team in the formation of a nucleus. The steps also contain suggestions on how to work with a kernel that has just been formed.

Steps to be completed (specify the start date, and the expected completion date)

6.1 Form a nucleus and have a commitment with its members. Start meetings for core members. Develop leadership in departments.

6.2 Develop strategy for small groups, choose a curriculum, and find leaders to take charge of them.

6.3 Ensure a meeting place, and confirm a date for the launch

6.4 Provide training for: The assimilation system, the ministry's servants, the team of praise ...

6.5 Create an investment process within the department; Recruit and train investment advisors.

6.6 Start meetings and mini-services before launch.

6.7 Create orientation class for newcomers.

6.8 Start classes for new children.

6.9 Develop a growth strategy over a two-year period.

Step 7: Launching a new church

Launching a new church. In the Bible, there is a certain public presence of a Christian assembly in Philippi. This is implied in two ways in the Scriptures. First, there is the very existence of the church at Philippi, to which Paul is going to write an epistle.

Second, there is reference to the implantation team during the prayer meeting, "as we went to the place of prayer." (Acts 16.16) The public launch is the date when the new assembly invites the community to participate in the weekly praise meetings. The implementation team and the nucleus will spend between three months and one year in preparation for this public launch.

Several nuclei have chosen to have public meetings before the official launch of the church weekly, monthly, and / or quarterly to verify the community's interest six to nine months before the public launch.

These pre-launch services are opportunities for the core to give a taste to the community's praise style, fraternal communion, and leadership direction of the implementation team. Pre-launch services are important. The enthusiasm generated during this pre-launch phase will tend to have a catalytic effect or a negative effect on the new congregation.

The following steps will help the Church's Mission Team understand and encourage the implementation team during the pre-launch activities.

These steps will also serve as a guide for the Implementation Team in preparing pre-launch activities, and in the actual launch date.

Steps to be followed (specify opposite the start date, and the expected completion date)

7.1 Implement a communication and public relations plan (create a logo, order business cards and stationery, produce materials to advertise, determine a timetable for the publication of newsletters, create a timetable for advertising, place an order to print material for personal relations, develop a new evangelistic brochure for the new church, send the first document by post, place several ads through several forms of media announcing the Sunday, etc.)

7.2 Clarify any financial or administrative matters (check bank accounts), establish procedures for custody of financial records, confirm receipt procedures, deal with legal matters and all matters pertaining to insurance, request an authorization to the post for a reduced price on the sending of letters in large quantity.

7.3 Plan of the first sermons and plan praise for the first quarter.

7.4 Develop a list of activities to be done for the LAUNCH Sunday and delegate tasks to the core members. (Check several times with the people who help in the nursery and in the children's ministry for LAUNCH Sunday.)

7.5 Check the equipment for the launch site and hire a team for the installation.

7.6 Complete all materials needed for first quarter services (to have more time to meet people before and after the launch Sunday).

7.7 Perform a rehearsal of the Sunday worship service of LAUNCH to eliminate any minor errors.

7.8 Develop a strategy for the first 100 days (share a few words with people on LAUNCH Sunday).

"Don't do it alone "

BIBLIOGRAPHY

1. Barclay, William, *The Master's men,* Publisher: Festival Books (June 1976), ISBN-13: 978-0687237326

2. Nicole, J. Marcel, *Précis d' histoire de l Église,* Librairie Chrétienne de Québec: #9782903100216

3. Evans, Tony, *God's Glorious Church: The Mystery and Mission of the Body of Christ,* Publisher: Moody Press, Chicago., ISBN13: 9780802439512

4. Guiteau, Gérald, *Le Pentecotisme en Haiti,* Imprimrie la Presse Evangélique,27 Blvd. Harry Truman, Port-au-prince, Haiti, ISBN:99935-2-169-8

5. Madistin, Samuel, *Le rôle du pouvoir législatif dans le fonctionnement modern de l'État,* Bibliothèque nationale d'Haiti,ISBN:99935-32-12-6

6. Bonnke, Reinhard, *Evangelism by Fire: Igniting Your Passion for the Lost,* 1990, W Publishing Group, ISBN-13: 9783935057196

7. *New Living Translation Bible,* Publisher: Tyndale House (March 1, 2006), ISBN-13: 978-1414309477

8. Pearlman, Myer, Le Manuel Du Pasteur, Editions Vida, ISBN-13: 978-0829710809

9. Rexroat, Stephen, *L'Esprit de l'école du dimanche,* Publisher Editions VIDA, 1983, ISBN 0882435949, 9780882435947

10. Thomas, Robert, *New American Standard Exhaustive Concordance of the Bible/Hebrew- Aramaic and Greek Dictionaries* -, Publisher: Holman Bible Pub (February 1981), ISBN-13: 978-0879811976

CPSIA information can be obtained
at www.ICGtesting.com
Printed in the USA
LVOW13s2231150617
538296LV00005BC/8/P